Fundamental Canine Obedience

Achieve Working Dog Performance For Your Dog

Tyler Hayes

East Coast Canine Inc.

Copyright © 2025 by Tyler Hayes

All rights reserved.

No portion of this book may be reproduced in any form without written permission from the publisher or author, except as permitted by U.S. copyright law.

www.eastcoastcanineinc.com

Contents

About the Author	VIII
Acknowledgements	X
Introduction	XIV
1. Equipment Orientation and Familiarization	1
The Flat Collar	
Martingale Collar	
Slip Chain Collar	
Prong Collar	
The Leash	
Equipment Conditioning	
2. Guidelines for Successful Training	17
3. Training Theory & Concepts	25
The Mind of the Dog	
Understanding the Dog's Drive	
Rewarding the Dog	
Correcting the Dog	
Timing of Reward and Correction	
Reward Marker Training	

4. Practical Training — 45
   A Note About Equipment
   Commands
   Moving Heel
   Right & Left Turns
   The Sit
   The Automatic Sit
   The Down
   The Stay
   The Recall
   The Finish

5. Training Structure & Exercises — 72
   What is Structured Obedience?
   Benefits of Structure in Training
   Equipment & Overview
   Exercise Principle
   Heelwork
   Walking Control
   Distance Control
   Introduction of Hand Signals
   The Down Hand Signal
   The Sit Hand Signal
   The Recall Hand Signal
   The Stay Hand Signal

6. Going Off-leash — 101
   Off-Leash Heelwork

    Off-Leash Walking Control
    Off-Leash Distance Control
    Continuing Off-Leash Training

7. Putting it All Together   121
    Benefits of Using a Training Course
    Building the Course
    Course Example - Layout
    Training Session Length
    Working Through the Course
    Course Examples - Heelwork
    Course Examples - Walking Control
    Course Examples - Distance Control

8. Advanced Theory & Practices   138
    Spontaneous Rewarding
    Dopamine and the Variable Reward
    Dog Decisions
    Introducing Distractions
    Problem Solving

9. Conclusion   154

Disclaimer   156

Training Notes   157

About the Author

Tyler Hayes is an experienced police canine handler as well as a certified Law Enforcement Canine Trainer. He is also a certified Law Enforcement General Instructor, and holds an Advanced Law Enforcement Certificate from the state of North Carolina. He, along with mentor and business partner Tim Braddy, own and operate East Coast Canine Inc. located in eastern North Carolina. Tyler has had the opportunity to train canines and canine handlers for many law enforcement agencies across the United States. Tyler has served as a K9 Handler in the Patrol Division and Special Operations Division of his law enforcement agency. During his time in the Special Operations Division he was assigned to the Violent Criminal Apprehension Team (VCAT). Tyler has conducted numerous K9 operations with many federal, state, and local law enforcement agencies to include: The Federal Bureau of Investigation SWAT, The U.S. Marshals Service, The U.S. Drug Enforcement Administration, The U.S. Postal Inspection Service, NC Alcohol Law Enforcement, NC Highway Patrol, and the NC Department of Public Safety. Tyler is a member of the United

States Police Canine Association (USPCA) where he also serves as a Region 2 Trial Judge.

Senior Police Officer T. Hayes & K9 Boone

Acknowledgements

My Wife - Your support of this project is unmatched. You kept me focused and tolerated many hours of me being away. This could have never been accomplished without you by my side. I love you dearly.

Mom - You are and will forever be a lifelong inspiration. I love you.

Tim Braddy - If it weren't for you I wouldn't even know which end of the leash to hold! There are more things to thank you for than there are pages to write on. You and Pam are absolute family. I love both of you.

Capt. Robert Rothrock - Your career advice and guidance will never go unappreciated. Thank you for believing in me.

Lt. M. H. Whitley (Ret.) - Thank you for your support and a friendship that will no doubt last a lifetime.

Anthony Puckett – Thank you for your friendship and contribution.

ACKNOWLEDGEMENTS

Ken Mathias - Thank you for your time, knowledge, and many lengthy conversations.

Pastor Andy Raynor - Thank you for your constant guidance and friendship.

A righteous man regardeth the life of his beast
Proverbs 12:10

To my son Knox with love.

Introduction

Whether you're a professional canine handler or you're simply seeking the best for your pet companion; the foundation to everything you do with your dog is obedience. The building blocks of obedience will be used to construct the foundation for the structure of every other task that you train your canine to do.

There have been an endless number of times throughout my career as a police canine handler where I can recall basic canine obedience playing a huge role in the success of an operation. At many times during high stress situations, I would have to call upon my canine partner to perform tasks that go completely against his internal instinct. Tasks such as remaining still and quiet while other officers maneuvered around a structure, recalling him back to my side after initially having sent him to apprehend a suspect, or having him leap into the window of a structure and then laying still until I could join him inside, as well as many others. None of these tasks would have ever been possible had he not had a firm foundation of obedience training, as well as a strong desire to want to perform.

As you journey through this book, you will learn the skills needed to train your dog to not only perform the basic fundamental obedience tasks, but also to enjoy doing it. Along the way you will learn the theory behind the training methods we will be using, as well as how to increase the drive and desire in your dog to perform the tasks that you are asking of him. All of the training in this book will require patience of the handler, as well as regular repetition of training sessions. There is no one-and-done canine training method. You, the handler, have to be willing to put in the time and effort into training your dog. Obedience is a perishable skill. Remember, you are training what would otherwise be a wild animal, who would embrace its natural instincts and primal instincts if it did not have a handler leading and conditioning him. As the handler you are up against those instincts, and it is your job to redirect that internal drive – in a positive manner – into avenues that will allow the canine to retain that same drive while also performing the learned tasks. Even if you have an older and more experienced dog, you can never overdo the basics. Dogs at all levels can benefit greatly from basic obedience training.

A bond between handler and dog isn't something that comes immediately, or at times even easy. A bond is built with trust, and trust is gained with experience. With time, dedication, and repetition, you can and will have a dog that is obedient, loyal, and reliable. Nothing strengthens the trust and bond between dog and handler more than regular obedience training.

Chapter One

Equipment Orientation and Familiarization

In the canine world there is an abundance of equipment available for your dog. There are many types of collars, leashes, and harnesses out there. Some of this equipment is very useful for canine training, while other items are mere gimmicks, completely impractical, and will work contrary to the obedient behavior that you are trying to achieve with your dog. Throughout this chapter we will look at different types of collars and leashes, and discuss the proper use and function of each, so that you can choose the one that works the best for your canine.

Before we get into the equipment that we will be using in this training I feel it necessary to talk about the various items to avoid. These are items that I am very much against when it comes to canine training. In my professional opinion, these pieces of equipment offer little to no structure to the dog and thus create bad habits within the dog that become much harder to remedy as time goes on.

For starters, any kind of leash that is designed to give leeway to the canine, such as a bungee leash, should never be used. These leashes may seem like they are easier on the dog or the handler, however, they allow the dog a certain amount of freedom at times when he decides to 'charge the leash' or pull away from the handler. In turn, this teaches the dog that he is allowed to carry on with this sort of behavior, and that all he has to do is pull harder to be able to get to whatever it is that he is trying for. The bungee leash also hinders the handler's ability to give a proper correction when needed, as again the leash will allot a certain amount of 'give' resulting in little to no correction to the dog.

The second type of leash to avoid is a retractable leash. On the surface, these leashes appear to offer the mobility of a short leash along with the convenience of having a long line available at the press of a button. However, the mechanisms inside of these leashes are prone to failure, especially with larger and stronger dogs with a tougher temperament. The most important reason to avoid these leashes is, again, they provide little to no correction to the dog. We will discuss exactly what a proper correction is in the upcoming chapters. There can be a time and place for a retractable leash however, while training basic obedience there is no use for this piece of equipment.

Another item to avoid is a harness. Pet dog harnesses are marketed as being easier on the dog due to it applying less pressure on the neck. While this may be true to some degree, they afford the handler less control over the dog. This again encourages the dog to be comfortable with forging ahead of the handler or charging the leash – which as you will come to learn is an unfavored behavior in a dog, especially a working dog. Harnesses for working dogs should only be used for the specific working task they are intended for, such as tracking. At no point should any obedience training that is discussed in this book be conducted using a harness on the dog as means of guidance and correction. All obedience training prescribed in this book should be conducted with a proper collar and leash only. So what are the proper collars and leashes?

The Flat Collar

First we will talk about collars. The type of collar that usually comes to mind when someone hears "dog collar" is what would most commonly be referred to as the flat collar. The flat collar is typically made of leather, nylon, or a synthetic rubber material and is secured with a metal or plastic buckle. The fitting of this collar should be snug to the dog while also allowing the handler to easily place four fingers underneath the collar when it is attached. Once attached, the dog should not be able to easily slip his head out of it. The width of the collar should be suitable for the size of the dog that will be wearing it. A good rule of thumb is: The larger the dog, the wider the collar. For working larger and stronger dog breeds such as the German Shepherd or Belgian Malinois, I would recommend a one and 1 1/4 inch up to a 2 inch-wide collar that is made of nylon or leather, and is secured using a metal buckle. These size and material combinations have been proven to be the most secure types of flat collars for the working dog.

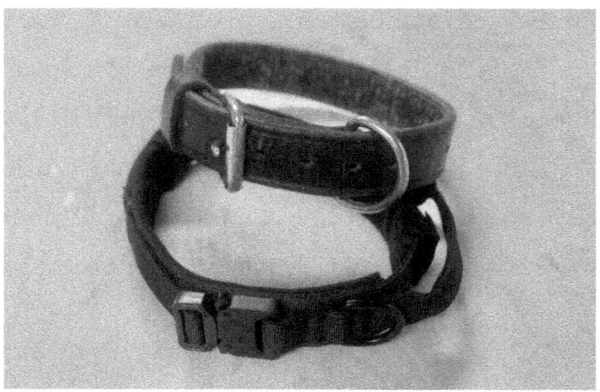

The flat collar should not be the only or primary means in which the handler secures and controls the dog. The flat collar is best used when there is a working task to be completed by the dog, such as a narcotic sniff, article search, or building search. In those instances the flat collar will allow the handler to have leash control of the dog while also allowing the dog to work freely. This will decrease the chance of the dog getting an unwarranted correction, which may otherwise distract or deter the dog from correctly performing the task. It has always been my practice and recommendation the flat collar only be placed on the dog when there is a task to be completed. This method results in the dog associating work with the collar. The dog then becomes aware that he is expected to work when the collar is placed on him. In most cases, once the dog has made this connection you will see the dog become excited just by the mere sight of the collar, and he will become extremely eager to work once it is placed on him.

While the flat collar offers the handler a great deal of control over the dog, it provides little to no practical method for correcting the dog. This is why I do not recommend the flat collar as the primary means of control during obedience training. Any attempted correction using a flat collar would most often be inconsistent and ineffective. Larger working dog breeds that naturally high-drive will quickly grow used to any pressure from the flat collar rendering it almost useless at correcting unwanted behavior. Moving forward in this chapter we will look at other options for collars that are better suited for obedience training.

Martingale Collar

The next collar we will discuss is the martingale collar. This collar has a similar look and feel as a flat collar, however it functions slightly differently. The martingale collar offers a limited-slip function. This function allows the collar to constrict slightly around the dog's neck whenever pressure is applied by way of the leash, or in the event that the dog attempts to maneuver in a manner that is contrary to the direction of the handler. One of the biggest advantages to this type of function is that it prevents the dog from being able to 'back out' of the collar in the event that he attempts to pull away from the handler. I find this function to be especially beneficial in the beginning stages of introducing the leash to the dog. The collar should be fitted to the dog in the same manner as the flat collar.

Additionally, the martingale collar offers a less-aggressive form of correction by limiting the level of constriction the collar can have on the dog. This collar should be operated with slight leash pressure only, and is not intended to be used for more intense corrections. The martingale collar is easy to use and can be an especially helpful tool for a novice dog handler or pet dog owner. Because of the collar's limited-slip function, it is very safe for the dog and does not require the handler to have extensive training to operate it.

This collar is my preferred collar to use when training puppies as the limited level of pressure it offers is not overly intimidating to a young dog with little to no collar and leash experience. With its non-aggressive appearance, this type of collar is also a great option for a more mild-tempered working dog, such as a police therapy dog. Overall, the martingale collar offers the look and feel of a flat collar while allowing the handler to have a slightly increased, yet comfortable, level of control over the dog.

Slip Chain Collar

One of the most effective collars available for canine obedience training is the slip chain collar, or what is sometimes referred to as the choke chain collar. This type of collar has historically been, and continues to be, the preferred collar for working dogs. In my time of handling and training canines I have found this to be the best tool for obedience training. The training that is to be discussed in this book is largely focused on working the canine with this style of collar. Essentially, the slip chain will be the gas pedal and brake that you use for working and training your dog.

The fitting should be so that the chain easily goes over the dog's head while at the same time not being so loose that it falls to his ears when his head is in a down position. If the slip chain hangs down to the dog's chest area, it is too large. The slip chain is sized based on length in inches, and link size in millimeters. The larger the link of the slip chain, the easier it is on the fur of the dog. The smaller links have a tendency to damage the fur around the neck of the dog, especially those with longer hair. I recommend a slip chain with a 3 to 4mm size link to it. Another option is the large link slip chain that is commonly referred to as the "fur saver" slip chain.

Despite its harsh-sounding name, the slip chain is by nature one of the most fair and efficient tools used for dog training. This collar allows for a correction to be given quickly to the dog and provides an immediate release of correction when pressure is lessened. The slip chain also allows for multiple levels of corrections, ranging from soft to stern, to be efficiently and easily given. It also gives the handler the ability to make corrections from multiple positions due to its ability to quickly adapt to handler and dog position. The slip chain has two rings attached to the chain itself: When properly fitted, one ring known as the 'live ring' allows for a slipping movement to occur, while the other ring known as the 'dead ring' provides the collar the ability to work in the same manner that a flat collar does. This is great flexibility to have because it allows for the handler to adjust the level of the collar's ability to give correction to the dog's behavior or task at hand. An example of this would be the handler having the leash attached to the live ring while walking the dog up to an area where he is going to conduct a detection sniff. Once at that area, the handler would detach the leash from the live ring and attach it to the dead ring prior to giving the dog the command to search. Being that the leash would now be attached to the dead ring, this would allow the handler to maintain a level of control over the dog while still providing the dog the opportunity to work without the risk of being corrected off of the task at hand.

Prong Collar

The prong collar functions similarly to the slip chain collar in that it has a live ring and a dead ring to it, and corrections are given in the same manner. While slip chain collars need to be fitted by length (i.e., 20 inches long, etc.) Prong collars are fitted by size (small, medium, large, or extra large). They all come in a standard length which is adjusted to fit the neck of the dog by removing or adding links to the collar. The correct fit and position for a prong collar is for it to sit right behind the ears and up under the jawline snugly. It should take minimal leash pressure to engage the pressure of the collar. A common problem new handlers tend to have is they don't remove enough links to get the correct snug fit. When that happens the collar hangs down on the dog's neck which results in the collar not working the way that it was designed to. The collar should be put on and taken off by pinching on of the links and slipping it apart. Do not attempt to push the collar over the dog's head to put it on or slip it off. An important thing to note with the prong collar is that it is meant to be put on for training and working the dog only. This collar should be removed when the dog is going to be placed into the kennel for the night or when the dog will be left alone for long periods of time. Failure to remove the collar during these times can result in irritation to the dog's skin or other injuries.

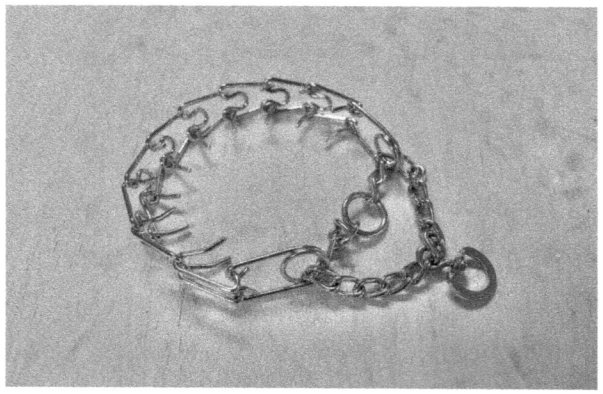

As mentioned, using the collar is similar to the use of the slip chain collar. When the leash is attached to the live ring the collar will contract when a correction is given. When the leash is attached to the dead ring the dog will meet the resistance of the prongs only without any constriction. I am reserved in my use of the prong collar for training. I typically only choose to use it for certain types of cases. Such a case may be if I am training a smaller-framed handler who has a larger and stronger dog where the handler is unable to make efficient corrections using the slip chain. This will typically resolve the issue due to the fact that the prong collar offers more of a correction with less of the effort. Another example would be if I am working with an overly-aggressive dog. The prompt response of the prong collar will quickly let the dog know that any sudden unwanted aggressive movement will invoke a correction.

The prong collar can be a true asset in dog training, especially during times of problem solving and behavior shaping. Fit and function are key to the use of the prong collar. Before using a prong collar on your dog, be sure to take the time to become familiar with the use and function of the one that you have. This will ensure the best training for your dog.

There are many other styles of collars on the market nowadays. However, I have found the collars mentioned above are the most practical and efficient options for working and training dogs, and I use them on a regular basis in my profession. As with every piece of training equipment that we discuss, proper fitting and proper use are key to ensuring the success of your canine's obedience training. A good rule of thumb is: If you are not yet comfortable with it, don't put it on your dog.

The Leash

Without a leash attached to it, the collar is only good for holding the name tag of a dog. The leash will be the steering wheel that you will use to guide your dog while teaching the desired behavior. Dog owners who have no formal education in dog training often view the leash as only a device that prevents the dog from running away. Admittingly, I have been guilty of this myself in the past. Prior to becoming a police canine handler I had only ever trained my own pet dog. Formal obedience was nowhere in my vocabulary, and I didn't mind if my dog pulled on the leash while walking because it was all I had ever known a dog to do. To me, a leash was only necessary to keep the dog within close proximity. It wasn't until years later when I was selected by my agency to be a police canine handler, and had started a basic canine handler school, that I became aware of just how important of a tool that a leash is in canine obedience training.

Leashes, like collars, come in all different sizes and materials. While a large portion of selecting a leash can be based on personal preference, a small part has to be chosen based on dog size and use. For instance, you wouldn't want to use a heavy one-inch wide thick leather leash for training a six-month-old Labrador puppy. The weight of the leash would be a hindrance to the dog during any level of training. You also wouldn't want to attempt to conduct obedience training with an uncharacteristically short leash, as this would not allow the dog the flexibility to make choices while training. Which, in turn, would interrupt his ability to learn.

EQUIPMENT ORIENTATION AND FAMILIARIZATION

When it comes to leashes, my personal preference for material is high quality leather. There are other leash material options such as nylon and synthetic, but I have found leather (when properly maintained) lasts incredibly long and tends to not pick up debris such as thorns or twigs during use. Leash material will be one of complete personal preference though; You will have to choose what best works for you as a handler. I strongly recommend the leash be a six-foot-long leash with a sturdy metal quick release clasp at the end. This is an easily manageable length of leash that at times when needed, gives the dog enough distance and space to freely perform a task or roam.

Proper management of the leash is one of the most important things that you can learn as a canine handler. When I am teaching a basic law enforcement canine handler school I will usually spend a day teaching what I like to call "leash choreography." Choreography itself can be defined as the art of designing sequences of movements of physical bodies, in which motion or form or both are specified. Choreography is dance, and dance is disciplined movement. In order to have proper leash management you must have structure. Efficient leash management is a key component in training your dog. You want your leash movements to be purposeful in all that you do, so as to not create bad habits in your dog. For instance, when training for the "sit" command leash pressure will need to be applied firmly and in the correct direction that you are wanting to dog to move for the task. If these movements are not structured and the leash is used incorrectly, the dog will not understand the task that you are trying to teach him.

The first step to address when it comes to leash management is how to properly hold the leash. To do this you will take your right thumb and place it through the loop on the end of the leash. Using your left hand you will then take up slack from the leash and loop it over your right thumb going from inside to out. You will then use your right hand to grip all parts that are hanging from your right thumb. Your left hand will be placed lower on the leash to manage the remaining part. See the figures below for clarification. Hand placement on leash can be switched for those who wish to heel their dog on the right side. This method of holding the leash is not only the safest way to hold it, but it is also the most effective for controlling and guiding the dog. For those in law enforcement, this method will allow you to quickly drop all of the leash in your right hand in the event that you need to access your weapon quickly. In doing so, you will still be holding the leash and controlling the dog with your left hand. It is important that when holding the leash you do not place the loop around your wrist or bundle the leash up

EQUIPMENT ORIENTATION AND FAMILIARIZATION 15

in your hands; doing so can result in injury. We will discuss leash management more in depth in the coming chapters as we learn to apply it in various obedience tasks.

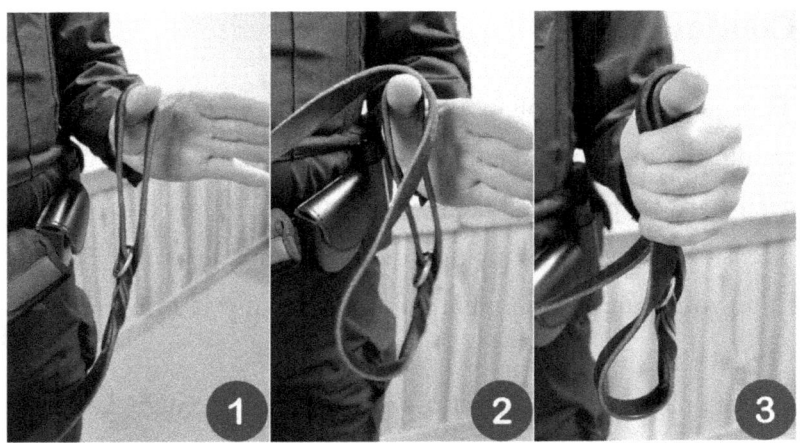

Equipment Conditioning

Prior to conducting any training actions with any of the equipment that you will be using with your dog, you should have a period of conditioning your dog to the equipment itself. The easiest way to accomplish this is to place the equipment on your dog and allow them to roam freely while taking time to play with them. This will help with any uneasiness they experience from having something new attached to them. Failure to properly condition your dog to any new equipment can result in them having a permanent negative view of the equipment. This can lead to nervous or aggressive behavior which in-turn will hinder your ability to conduct obedience training.

Conclusion

Throughout this chapter we have discussed a wide range of canine training equipment. Like any other tool that you would buy, you'll get what you pay for. Take the time to research products so as to ensure that you are buying a quality reputable brand. The last thing you want is equipment failure, especially at a time when it counts the most.

The proper fit and correct use of your equipment are key components when it comes to training your dog. These components can make or break your dog when it comes to obedience training. Remember, the collar is the gas pedal and brake, and the leash is the steering wheel. In the coming chapter we will focus on you, the driver, and making sure you have the knowledge that you need to properly navigate your dog's obedience training.

Chapter Two

Guidelines for Successful Training

As you will come to see when we get into practical training, with all that we do with dogs, there must be structure. Guidelines provide us with the framework for that structure. In this chapter you will learn the basic rules of canine training. From this point forward, these rules should be applied every time you conduct a training session with your dog.

Always begin and end training on a positive note.

When you first get the dog out, take a moment to pet him. Speak with him in a positive and exciting tone saying things like "Good dog!" The dog will not be concerned with the training about to take place, he will simply be happy to be with you.

When finished with the training session have him complete one task such as a sit, or recall, and reward him and praise him in abundance. You can even jog with him back to his kennel while telling him "good boy!" this will help him be more attentive to you during the training session and in turn aid in strengthening the bond.

Training at times will be tough for him as you will be applying pressure to him at various points during the session. Ending on a solid positive note will give the dog a sense of accomplishment and make him eager to train again the next time.

K9 Korado - Currituck County Sheriff's Office

Do not attempt too much too soon.

Focus on one task at the time when it comes to training for each command. Never attempt to condition two behaviors at the same time. For example, you wouldn't attempt to teach your dog to heel and lay down at the same time. The pressure used with one will affect the other. In this example you would train your dog to heel and once he was proficient at that, you would move on to train him to lay down. Condition them apart from each other and then put them together. Once he is proficient at both down and heel you could put both exercises together in the same session. Train to get one task to be top notch prior to moving on to the next. This will aid in building confidence and a solid foundation within the dog.

Keep training sessions short.

Training sessions should be short enough that the dog can see the light at the end of the tunnel. Extended training sessions typically lead to poor performance by the dog. This is usually due to the dog becoming tired or losing interest in the activities that are going on. A good rule of thumb is to keep the training sessions to around 30 minutes or less at a time. This will not only aid in keeping the dogs energy and attention up, but it again will leave the dog wanting more. Thus, setting up your next training session for success.

Time in between sessions should be approximately an hour or more. This allows the dog time in the "think tank": Immediately following a training session the dog should be placed back in his kennel, where he should remain until the next training or play session. This gives the dog time to ponder his last experience, and allows him time to become eager for the next.

Balance pressure and praise.

Anytime a correction is given, it should be matched with an equal or higher level of praise once the task is accomplished. Dogs have about the same mind capacity and processing as a three year old child. The level of excitement and energy that you would give a child who just showed you their scribble art should be the same that you give your dog when he sits on command. Always remember: praise will be the glue that bonds you and your dog together!

Never compare your dog to another dog.

Dogs share similar traits and characteristics in their personality and trainability. However, each dog will have its own individual strengths and weaknesses when it comes to abilities. Thus, some types of training will require more time with one dog versus another. For instance, when I am training a class of law enforcement dogs and handlers, I may find that one dog responds to tracking training more slowly than the others and another dog responds to detection training more slowly than the others. While both dogs will become successful working dogs, additional training time will likely be needed in the areas in which they are developing at a lower pace.

Whether you're training with a class, a working unit, or with another friend, keep in mind that all dogs learn at their own pace.

This is why it's important not to compare and contrast the progress of your dog to another.

East Coast Canine Basic K9 Handler Class 2024-3

Change training locations often.

We have all heard the story of the family that moves to a new house miles away from their former home. Not long after moving in, the dog goes missing and they end up finding it back at their old house. Dogs have a keen sense of smell and will develop conditioned responses to smells, whether by formal training or primal response. A dog will naturally come to know that home is home based on this conditioning. This is the same for training areas. If you only ever train your dog in one particular location, then he will come to know what is expected from him in that area. Changing up the training area from time to time will help condition the dog to know that obedience is expected from him in every area and not just at a certain location and time.

Make training fun.

What you expose the dog to just before and just after a training session is as important as the training session itself. We always say to end training on a positive experience, however it is just as important to begin training on a positive experience. Start small and end small. Start with a basic command that the dog is familiar with and no matter how complex the training session is, end with that same simple command and lots of fun.

In order to get the best performance from your dog he has to have the desire to perform the tasks that you are asking of him. While there are multiple elements that factor into the drive of a dog, pleasure is of the most importance when it comes to training. The dog has to *want* to work. This *want* comes from creating a fun atmosphere for training. The more fun you make it, the more he will want to do it. We will get deeper into how to make it fun in the coming chapters.

K9 Boone - Rocky Mount Police Department

Keep a Positive Attitude

We have a saying in the police K9 world: "It all runs down leash." What we are referring to is the attitude of the handler. If not already, you and your dog will develop such a bond that he will be in tune with your emotions and attitude. In turn, your dog feeds off of your energy and composure. If you are frustrated he will feel this same frustration, which can cause nervousness in the dog, resulting in a lesser performance than usual.

Training a dog can be an exhausting activity. Not only physically, but emotionally as well. We desire the best for our dogs and this includes the best performance of our dogs. We have to understand that training takes time and repetition. When a moment arises where our dog is not performing to the standard that we have set in our mind, we have to pause and reset. Don't act out of frustration. Any action toward your dog rooted in frustration will ultimately work against the progress you have made in your training. When it comes to training sessions with your dog remember: Be positive to receive positive.

K9 Clyde - Rocky Mount Police Department

Chapter Three

Training Theory & Concepts

A simple Google search of "dog training methods" will produce a never-ending abundance of articles, videos, and opinions. One could get lost for days in this overwhelming amount of content. It would be easy for a person to become incredibly confused as to what to trust, as each will claim to be the best method for training your dog. While the internet can be a great resource it can also be a major hindrance. Anyone online can claim to be a dog trainer and have an instant audience. This does not always mean that what is being said is true. Avoid falling for tricks and gimmicks. Year after year I see new terminology being created to describe methods that have been around for decades, all in an effort to sell a product or service. Anything claiming to be the latest and greatest in dog training should be approached with caution. Dog training in its simplest form is this: good behavior gets rewarded, and bad behavior gets corrected.

In an effort to avoid creating that same overwhelming feeling for the reader of this book, I will not be discussing every method of dog training that has been theorized over the years. I will be focusing exclusively on the methods that I, along with other staff at East Coast Canine Inc., routinely use. These methods are not overly complicated, and have repeatedly proven to be effective and successful.

The Mind of the Dog

To set you, the handler, up for the best success in implementing these training methods, we must first examine the dog's ability to learn. You wouldn't attempt to teach toddlers quantum physics any more than you would attempt to teach graduate students how to crawl. Both scenarios would receive the same reaction... confusion.

When it comes to dog training, instruction has to be given at a level the dog can comprehend. The same applies to the objective itself; The task you are wanting to train your dog to do has to be a task that is at, or around, his current level of training. The first step to understanding how a dog learns is to consider the mind of the dog. Knowing how the dog's mind works will give you an understanding of how to approach the dog in training.

K9 Astro - Johnston County Sheriff's Office

It is best to view the canine's mental capacity as being roughly 90% memory and about 10% other. With such a large portion of the mind being memory, it is safe to say that in dogs, memory is the equivalent to intelligence. The better the capacity for memory, the more intelligent the dog will appear to be. The saying goes that if you want to know what a dog has in its memory, watch it behave. Take an in-house dog for instance; He will know whether he is allowed on the couch or not. This is not based on his understanding that the couch is a couch and people sit there not dogs, but rather his recollection of what is associated with the couch. If every time he attempted to get on the couch he was given a correction then he will recall through memory that couch equals correction. However, if every time the dog hops on the couch he gets belly rubs from his owner, he will recall through memory that the couch equals a pleasant experience.

This same memory recollection is what we rely on when it comes to training the dog. We attempt to condition the dog, not teach it. "Conditioning" requires only active sensory receptor organs and a good memory. "Learning" requires the ability to reason, and the ability to interpret mental images to discover abstract properties. Dogs lack these abilities and so cannot accomplish advanced learning. This is why in training, we do not place the dog in a position where he must reason, apply logic, or perform any mental function beyond memory and recall. Doing so sets the dog up for obvious failure. If anything, you as the handler should be at ease knowing that your job is only to provide consistent conditioning to the dog and nothing more beyond that. Understand that there is nothing new in dogs. A dog born today has the same mental capacity and functional limitations as the first dog that the Lord placed upon on earth. With all of this in mind, the next logical question would be "what makes the dog want to work?"

Understanding the Dog's Drive

There are many things that factor into what motivates a dog to perform. For professional canine trainers we collectively measure those motivators under the term 'drive'. When sourcing potential working dogs, we will conduct a series of tests with each prospective dog in order to determine the level of drive that the dog has. Drive does not simply refer to whether a dog is an energetic dog or not, but rather the dog's workability and focus. Dogs that are going to be used for specific tasks have to possess the appropriate drive for the job that they are going to be doing. That appropriate level of drive has to be in place not only for the training of the desired task, but also for the later performance of those tasks. For instance, if I am selecting a dog for law enforcement work, one that will track persons and detect narcotic or explosive odor, I will be looking for one with a strong drive for hunting. I will conduct specific tests to determine how long and to what lengths the dog will search for a particular item of interest, such as a toy, that he likes. On the other hand if I am selecting a dog to be a therapy dog then I want to find one who has low, or even little to no hunting drive, as his work will not require such skills. Think about this in terms of vehicles. If you are going to choose a vehicle to pull a utility trailer with, you are going to want a vehicle with a strong engine. While a Ford F250 truck and a Chevrolet Corvette car both have strong engines, one of the two is better equipped for the particular task at hand.

K9 Omar - Currituck County Sheriff's Office

So how does understanding what drive is help you in training your dog? Well, to go anywhere you need fuel for the drive. Knowing what drive is helps you, the handler, to determine just what it is that your dog is working for, and also helps you in determining how to use this to your advantage when it comes to training for a particular goal.

Rewarding the Dog

Before we go any further it is very important for you to know: Dogs do not work to please their handler, they work to obtain a reward from the handler. As simple as it may sound, the remaining training that you will do with your dog from this point forward hinges upon a true understanding of that statement. You may be thinking "What about the bond?" The bond is important, but it is not the 'why' to the dog's drive.

TRAINING THEORY & CONCEPTS

K9 Bolt - Saxonburg Police Department

Think about this in terms of your job. Let's imagine that you work a job you truly love. This is a job where every day your tasks bring you absolute joy. Even if that were the case, you wouldn't show up to work week after week for the sole purpose of pleasing your boss at this job. You would, however, show up week after week for the reward your company is going to give you for doing that job, especially when the reward is money. Sure, pleasing your boss is a part of the process but it's not the point of the process. The point of the process is to achieve your reward. In this scenario, you have a drive (passion and motivation) for the work of your job, which is further fueled by knowing you are going to receive a reward (paycheck) at the completion of your weekly job related t asks.

This is the same manner in which tasks appear to the dog. He may have the type of drive that allows him to be an outstanding tracking dog, and he may appear to you his absolute happiest when he is tracking a person. However, what is really on his mind isn't the chance of making the case of the century by locating the bad guy, rather it is the reward that he knows is coming when he completes this task.

By now you may be asking "What is the reward?" The reward is simply whatever the dog chooses for it to be. By this I mean that it's something the dog strongly prefers, to the point that he may prefer it over anything else. Rewards should appeal to one of three areas of the dog's life: hunger, affection, or play.

One of the first things that comes to mind when discussing rewards is food. Food can be a good choice for initially beginning reward-based training. I especially like to use food in the early stages of training puppies. When using food to reward you should use very small pieces. Food is a low-value reward, meaning that you can only go so far with it when training. Once the dog is full, the value of the reward is significantly lowered.

Appealing to the affection of the dog should be done by using a combination of voice and touch in order to 'praise' the dog. Praise should be given after every successfully-completed task. Phrases like "good boy" should be spoken to the dog in a higher pitched voice with a happier tone. This is done in order to allow the dog to differentiate between a command, a vocal correction, and praise. Commands and vocal corrections should be given in a voice that is normal tone to slightly stern. While they won't understand your words when praising them, dogs will most often immediately respond to your happier and higher-pitched voice tone. Give these types of vocal praise while petting and scratching them and you'll end up with one happy dog.

The reward most often used for working dogs is the one that appeals to the dog's desire to well... be a dog! The 'play' reward is one of the best types of rewards to use. This involves rewarding the dog with his favorite toy and then playing with him using it. This can be in the form of a ball or bumper that is used for fetch, or a tug toy that you can use to play tug-of-war with. When it comes to toys some dogs can be very child-like in their choosing. You may find that one dog likes ball-type toys more so than tug-style toys. If a dog does not initially take interest in one toy then try several others. If there is still a lack of enthusiasm, try rolling the toy across the ground. This can provoke the prey drive in the dog and cause him to want to chase after the toy. You are the one who makes the toy interesting to the dog. Keep it moving either by fetch, rolling it, or playing tug with it, in order to hold the dog's attention. This will aid in building the toy drive within the dog. Unlike food, the toy reward is a high-value reward. A dog who loves his toy will always want to play with his toy.

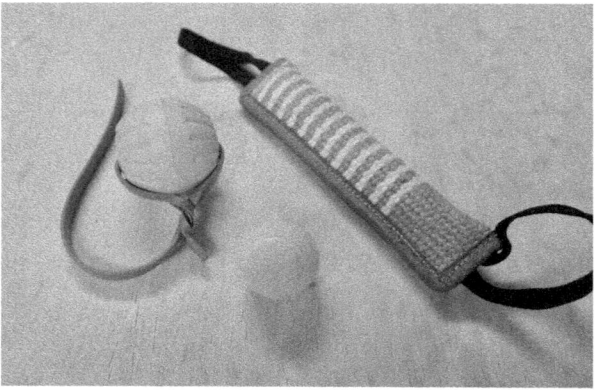

When rewarding the dog I recommend using a combination of toy and praise, food and praise, or at times praise alone. Using a combination of praise in conjunction with a toy or food will strengthen the dog's desire for either the toy or the food, and also aid in building the bond between dog and handler. Never use a combination of food and toy at the same time. Doing so typically lessens the dog's desire for one or the other. It is important to keep the interest of both rewards so that you can vary the reward during training.

Correcting the Dog

Up to this point we have discussed rewarding the dog. Rewarding is only one of the instruments that we will use in training the dog. The other method that we will employ is corrections. This is simply an introduction of an unpleasant experience to the dog. This is what we refer to as "giving a correction." Without the principle of discipline and reward there would be no training of dogs, or humans for that matter. Reward and correction are the hammer and chisel that we will use to sculpt the behavior of the dog.

Before we discuss corrections any further, let me first tell you what a correction is not. A correction is **not** a punishment. There is a clear and distinct difference in punishment and correction. The difference is that punishment is intended to extract some type of payment from an individual for transgressions committed; while a correction is intended to immediately deter an action and to condition a behavior. Let me be clear in saying that there is ***no room for punishment in dog training.*** Punishment only works in humans because we have the ability to understand and reason. Let's say that a man robs a bank, and it takes ten years for the man to be caught and sentenced to prison. The man can understand that he is being punished for something that he did ten years prior. Dogs lack this level of understanding and reason. Let's say a farmer's dog attacks and kills a chicken. Hours later the farmer finds the dog standing on the front porch and then scolds him. This will be ineffective. The dog will only associate standing on the porch with the punishment due to the amount of time that has passed and the fact that the dog can not reason crime and punishment. We will talk more about this when we discuss timing.

> **Corrections are designed to accomplish three things:**
>
> 1. Increase precision in the dog's performance;
>
> 2. Reduce the dependency on primary rewards such as food and toy;
>
> 3. Ensure that the dog performs the assigned task despite any distractions.

There are various types of corrections. For ease of understanding I have placed them into two categories: audible and physical. An audible correction can be something as simple as a simple "no" when the dog is heading in an undesired direction. It can also be a clap of the hands accompanied by a loud "Phooey!" when the dog is at a distance. For physical corrections I am speaking of leash corrections only. By this, I mean when the leash is attached to the collar. This can be a sudden jerk of the leash when the dog is attempting to dart away, or it may be a maintained pressure of the leash to get the dog to move into a certain position. A physical correction can also mean a removal of a physical element, such as praise. For instance, if the dog jumps up on you and you choose to ignore the dog and not give praise or petting. In this case the dog would learn that jumping on you is an unwanted behavior since it does not bring about the affection that he was hoping for.

There is nothing wrong with placing the dog in a position where he may be exposed to discomfort or undesired events. These are the kinds of things that motivate a dog to make a choice. If the dog continues to perform behavior which subjects him to the undesired aspects of training, then so be it. Sooner or later he will learn that there is a way to avoid it.

Before implementing corrections, it is important that you understand the following rules:

- **The dog must have the ability to perform the behavior that you are requesting.** Dogs register events in fairness. It would be unfair to the dog to command a behavior that he doesn't know, and then correct him when he doesn't perform it. Correct undesired behavior only in the event that you know the dog is performing in a manner that is contrary to his ability.

- **Do not increase corrections in order.** By this I mean don't start with a soft correction and get tougher and tougher if the dog does not abide the first time. Dogs, especially those who are high-drive and intent on obtaining a reward, can quickly build a tolerance to uncomfortable stimuli. Without meaning to, you can easily create a dog that is unmanageable; one who is highly motivated but unfazed by any level of correction due to the fact that he's been conditioned to absorb an enormous amount of physical discomfort. This is why it is imperative that you give a correction that is of an intensity that is meaningful to the dog and enough of a correction that it causes change to the behavior immediately. One good correction will do the job where many tentative ones fail.

- **<u>Avoid emotion when giving corrections.</u>** You should never give a correction out of frustration. Canine training has never been promised to be easy. There will be times when you may become overwhelmed. Even in teaching police canine handlers I have seen grown men shed tears due to being so frustrated with their dog's performance. Frustration is going to happen. However, your dog should never be an outlet for it. If during a training session you feel that you are getting frustrated, stop. Quit whatever you are working on and leave it for another day. Play with your dog for a few moments and then put him up until you can gather your thoughts and composure. Continuing to train when you are frustrated will only cause a decrease in performance with your dog.

The correction you choose to give should match the immediate behavior and experience of the dog. There will be an obvious difference in the correction given to the dog who is heading toward a fire pit versus the older and experienced dog who chooses not to sit the first time you tell him. You, the handler, should exercise maturity and understanding when it comes to choosing to correct an undesired behavior. Anytime you have had to give a high level of correction, or when you have had to give repeated corrections during a training session, remember that you always want to end on a good note with your dog. Take your dog and give him a simple task that he does well. When he performs, give him a lot of praise, petting, and affection. This will ease the pressure you have placed on the dog and will help keep the training fun for him.

Timing of Reward and Correction

When speaking about fashion, Vogue editor-in-chief Anna Wintour once said: *"It's all about timing. If it's too soon, no one understands. If it's too late, everyone's forgotten."* Now I'm no fashion guru, nor do I read Vogue magazine; however, when applied to dog training that quote holds an awful lot of value.

When it comes to conditioning a dog's behavior, there is truly nothing more important than correct timing. Training a dog for a specific behavior can lead to the weakening of another behavior and vice versa. This is why it is necessary for the handler to implement the proper action at precisely the right moment. Corrections or rewards implemented only a second too soon (or too late) from one exercise to the next can cause all levels of problems. The same is true for inconsistency of correction or reward from one task to the other. A dog will only associate his last behavior with your current reaction.

Think in terms of photography for a moment. We are always trying to capture that perfect family or group photo. The one where everyone is smiling and looking at the camera at the same time and no one is blinking. So we get everyone into frame by placing them where we need them. We tell them all to look forward and smile. Then we wait for the perfect moment when no one is blinking to quickly hit the shutter button, finally capturing the photo. This is the same logic that we will apply to rewards and corrections given to the dog. Think of the reward or correction as your shutter button to capture the photo of the desired or undesired behavior.

Let's say that you give your dog the command of 'sit' and he squats and hovers instead of coming to a complete sit. If you reward him when he squats and hovers you will have "captured" that behavior only. The dog will begin to think that he gets rewarded for a squat and hover instead of a complete sit. Furthermore, if you gave the command 'sit' and then rewarded the dog before he had a chance to sit, he would never learn the command. He would only think that he has to do nothing to receive his reward when you say the word "sit." The same goes for waiting too long to reward. If you give the dog the command 'sit' and he sits, but the reward is withheld for so long that the dog gets up and walks to you, and then you reward him, the behavior that will be captured is him coming to you. Not the sit.

For an example on how this works for corrections, let's go back to the scenario of the farmer's dog and the chicken. If the dog attacks a chicken and the farmer attempts to correct this, even if the dog has the chicken in his mouth, it will be too late. The dog has already obtained the prize that he wanted, and too much time has passed for him to logically understand the correction. Now let's say the farmer has the dog on a leash that is attached to a slip chain collar on the dog. The farmer walks the dog past the chicken house, and then gives him a jerk of the collar and says a firm "leave it" at the precise moment the dog begins to turn and move toward the chicken house. The farmer in this instance will have effectively "captured" the undesired behavior with the correction. Thus teaching the dog that moving toward the chickens will bring about a correction. Coupled with enough consistency, this training would teach the dog to leave the chickens alone.

Once again... timing is everything. So is the case with dog training. Remember, don't reward or correct too soon, or too late.

K9 Narco - Pikeville Police Department

Reward Marker Training

A reward marker is something your dog can perceive (a sound or word) that predicts that a reinforcer (reward) is coming. It is a powerful tool in training that can bring great clarity to your dog, allowing him to know and learn the specific behavior that you are rewarding him for. Use of a reward marker will make training incredibly effective; It will blur the lines between work and play making all activities fun for your dog.

Your reward marker should be a simple one-syllable word that you are most likely to say in nearly the same manner, no matter your excitement level. I have found that the word "yes" is the simplest and easiest word to use. This is what I will be referring to throughout the remainder of this book.

As previously mentioned, timing is everything when it comes to dog training. This is also the same for training with a reward marker. You must mark the behavior at the moment the correct behavior is displayed. This will be what lets your dog know exactly what you are wanting from him. Let's use the sit behavior for example. You will give your dog the command "sit"; as soon as his hind parts hit ground into the position you would say "yes" and then reward him.

When you use your verbal marker ("yes") you should not say anything else before it. For instance, when your dog comes to a sit, don't say "Good boy, yes!" or "Much better, yes!", you will simply say "yes".

It is equally as important that you do not reach for his reward until after you have given the reward marker. If you reach too soon, your dog will begin watching your hands resulting in him connecting your movement with the reward instead of his behavior with the reward.

Reward marker training has to flow smoothly in order for it to be effective in your dog's training. This flow should be uninterrupted and timely. As with all training methods, consistency is key. Once you implement reward marker training, it should carry on throughout the life of your dog, ensuring that your companion's obedience develops accurately and sharply.

Chapter Four

Practical Training

Up to this point we have discussed equipment, training guidelines, and understanding the dog. In this chapter we will be putting all of that into action. This is the section where you will begin to condition your dog's behavior into desired actions. Moving into this portion it's important to remember that dog training takes time, repetition, and most importantly, patience.

Throughout this chapter I aim to not only teach the action that will achieve the behavior from the dog that you desire, but also to provide you with some various problem solving methods. These methods can be a great help when dealing with any initial avoidance from your dog that you may experience during the the beginning stages of training each exercise.

It is of utmost importance that you only attempt to condition one behavior at a time. If you are working on the sit, then stick to training the sit until it is proficient. Once proficient, then move on to the next behavior that you are attempting to condition. Eventually, once your dog has mastered more than one skill, you can conduct obedience training in which you combine all of their skills during one session. We will talk more on this in a future chapter.

For any new exercise that you introduce to your dog, the first few training sessions should be kept fairly short so that your dog remembers what he has learned. Initially, two to three sessions a day will work well. Once your dog starts to catch on, the frequency and duration of your training sessions can increase. And remember, praise your dog frequently!

K9 Kadjar - Currituck County Sheriff's Office

A Note About Equipment

The actions and training methods described for each of these tasks will be focused around using the leash and the slip chain collar only. Prior to beginning these phases of training it is important that you condition your dog to the equipment that will be used. By this I mean that he should be accustomed to wearing the slip chain and having the leash attached.

To accomplish this conditioning you should first start with the slip chain collar alone. Place the slip chain collar on as described in the equipment section of this book. Once the collar is on, begin to play with him and pet him. This will allow him to begin to associate positive things with the collar itself. Allow your dog to wear the collar for a day or so without any use of its corrective function. This will get him accustomed to the feel of this particular collar.

If your dog has not spent much time on a leash, or if he has not had any structured training using the leash, he should be conditioned to the leash as well. To do this you will attach your leash to the live ring of the slip chain collar and allow the dog to roam freely. This will get him used to the feel of the weight of the leash on the collar. This will also allow him to gently learn the constricting action of the slip chain collar as well. If he shows any avoidance toward the leash at all such as him charging away from you in an attempt to 'get away' from it, or him shutting down by laying or sitting frozen in a fearful manner, then spend some time playing with him and petting him while the leash is on. This can even be done on a fifteen foot leash in order to give you distance for playing fetch with a toy while the leash is still on. This will help reassure him that the leash is a positive thing.

Conditioning should be done with any new piece of equipment that you will use to train your dog with. It should be done prior to any action or engagement with the equipment. You should strive to make the dog view the equipment as a positive thing. This will greatly improve the effectiveness of the equipment and the success of your training.

Commands

Every desired behavior must have an associated command. Dogs obviously do not understand words by definition however they will easily come to associate the word sound and tone with an action or non-action behavior. Commands can be completely of your choosing. Some handlers choose to train their dog in a language that is not native to their region. For instance, I have always chosen the Dutch language to use for commands for my working dogs. This was done for safety reasons so no one else could command my dog. For the purpose of working through this book, we'll be sticking to English commands. Below are the commands that we will use, along with the associated dog behavior we wish to train. Should you desire to train your dog in a different language, simply translate the words below to such language.

- **Heel** - The command for your dog to walk next to you.

- **Sit** - Your dog in a seated position.

- **Down** - Your dog laying down fully.

- **Stay** - Your dog remains in the last position you commanded.

- **Here** - Used to call your dog to you.

- **No/Nay** - Used when undesired behavior occurs.

- **Yes** - Used to mark desired behavior when it occurs.

- **Leave it** - Used when your dog becomes distracted by something.

- **Free** - A release word to allow your dog to play/roam freely.

You may substitute other words for the ones I have listed above. Whichever commands you choose to use, make sure you stick with that command from the beginning, so as not to confuse your dog later on.

Moving Heel

The moving heel is the first thing that I teach every dog that I train, and it is the first thing I have my law enforcement K9 handler students teach their dogs. It is important for the dog to be able to walk in a controlled manner with the handler, whether on or off leash. If they can't do this on leash, they will never be able to do it off leash. This is a very important foundation to build as it will determine your dog's behavior everytime he is attached to the leash. Everything you do with your dog beyond this will rest upon the tone of the training that you conduct with your dog while conditioning this behavior. With that in mind, let's begin.

K9 Bolt - Saxonburg Police Department

With your leash hooked to the live ring of the slip chain, begin with your dog on your left side. The excess leash should be held in the right hand as described in chapter one. Give the command "heel" and start walking straight forward stepping first with your left foot. The importance of stepping off with the left foot first has to do with the dog's understanding of non-verbal cues. As you progress in training, your dog will come to learn that when you walk away beginning with your left foot, he is to immediately follow you.

Do not continue to command the dog to "heel" once you have started the exercise. Give only one voice command. This will encourage your dog to respond to the one command, and not to wait for the second or third.

The initial reaction you get from your dog can vary and may be quite interesting. Your dog may be intimidated or over stimulated. In either case, your dog may demonstrate protest. We will work through both of these categories of behaviors. However, the goal is the same: To ignore the protest and continue the exercise. Your dog has to ultimately learn that he must sometimes do things that he doesn't want to do. So if you love your dog, let him learn this inescapable fact early and in the simplest way.

For the intimidated dog, the behavior may be in the form of planting his paws and attempting to stay in place, or it may be that he walks much further back from you. In this case the best action is to encourage your dog. In most cases this can be accomplished with verbal praise which will get his attention and assure him that everything is okay.

With the overstimulated dog, the protest may be in the form of charging ahead on the leash, or attempting to flee from you. In this case you should give a correction followed by an immediate redirection. Do this by giving a jerk of the leash and making a 180 degree 'about face' turn, continuing to walk forward in the new direction.

When you come to a stop, give the leash a small tug back and reward your dog when he stops. As you progress in training the moving heel you will want to demand precision from your dog. Should he swing his hind parts out away from you when you stop, reach down and pull him back into position beside you before praising him. Along with this progression, continue to use spontaneous 180 degree turns. This will continue to build your dog's attentiveness to your movements.

Right & Left Turns

Once your dog is proficient at the moving heel, and he sticks with you fairly well during 180 degree turns, you will be ready to implement right and left turns. In this stage of training you should make sharp 90 degree turns so as to teach your dog to move when you move. If the turns are too broad and soft, your dog will not be conditioned to stick with you during abrupt movements.

Having a dog that is conditioned to this extent is beneficial especially when it comes to being obedient around distractions such as other dogs or people. For the working dog, it is important to have this level of maneuverability for any tactical situations that may arise. The handler needs to be able to trust that his dog will stick with him no matter the movement.

To begin this conditioning, start with the right turn. With your dog at a moving heel, you should give the command "heel" and then make a sharp 90-degree right turn. At the same moment that you make your turn give a sharp jerk of the leash. This will cue your dog in to your action and thus change his course of movement. Repetitions of this exercise will show him that he is to move when you move. Do not make multiple sharp right turns in a row in attempts to condition your dog quicker. This will only lead to confusion and frustration in your dog. Instead, make the right turn and then continue straight forward with the moving heel for twenty or more steps before making another right turn. Doing so will give the dog the time to process the action that just occurred. This will condition the dog to be more attentive to your movements and to move when you do in order to avoid the correction.

Training for the right turn is typically easier than training for the left due to it being more fluid of a motion. As I've stated previously, we never attempt to condition more than one behavior at a time. Therefore, do not move to conditioning the left turn until your dog is proficient at the right turn.

To begin the left turn, you will start at a moving heel. Just prior to making a sharp left turn you will move your left hand down lower on the leash toward the dog. Give the command "heel" and then make a sharp 90-degree left turn. At the time that you make a left turn, sharply pull back on the leash with your left hand.

Maintain back pressure to the collar through the duration of the left turn. Immediately continue forward with a moving heel.

If you perform this left turn maneuver and the dog continues to push forward while you are turning, you should walk directly into your dog. After making the left turn, push forward no matter what. Even if initially this requires you to 'walk through' your dog as he attempts to continue to move in the opposing direction. This will force your dog to reposition himself in order to avoid the collision. This will result in your dog paying closer attention to you so that he can get out of your way and turn with you.

Though the application is different, the left turn will require the same repetition and timing as the right turn. You should conduct the left turn exercise and then continue twenty or more paces before performing another left turn maneuver. Once this behavior is successfully conditioned, you can begin to integrate both right and left turns into your obedience training sessions.

Once your dog shows proficiency at both right and left turns by requiring little to no corrective actions, discontinue the "heel" command prior to the turns. Continue training both turns. As with all training, be sure to give your dog a reward and lots of praise for his good work. Soon your dog will be attentive to your movement and will be turning with ease.

K9 Ares - Jackson County Sheriff's Office

The Sit

The next exercise for your dog to learn will be the sit. The sit will set the tone for all other non-moving behaviors that you will teach your dog. As with all exercises, be sure to show your dog exactly what you are wanting him to do.

To begin, start with your dog at the heel position on your left side. Give the command 'sit'. At the same time, using your right hand on the leash, pull straight up. Maintain this upward tension with the leash while using your left hand on your dog's hindquarters to press firmly downward, encouraging him to sit. As soon as your dog has reached a complete sit, mark the behavior with "yes" and then reward him with his toy and praise.

K9 Bolt - Saxonburg Police Department

All of these steps, while many, should be conducted in one fluid motion once the command of 'sit' is given. Timing is of the utmost importance here. There should be less than a second between the given command, and the leash action with hand press. This is what will allow the dog to begin to understand the meaning of the word itself.

In the beginning stages of this conditioning, your dog may exhibit a number of different resistant behaviors. For instance, your dog may begin to squat in a sitting motion and then pop back up to a stand before coming to a complete sit. Should this happen, give your dog a firm "no", and then proceed with the command and steps once more, making sure to follow through. Another possibility is your dog not coming to a complete sit. In this case the dog would squat and hover instead of coming fully down to a sit position. Should this happen, re-apply the upward leash pressure and downward pressure on the hindquarters until the completed sit is achieved. If you allow your dog to not fully sit now, he will never want to come to a complete sit later.

Another possibility during the initial stages of training is that your dog may sit off from you at an angle. If this happens simply use your left hand to reach over him and place your palm on his left hind area. Then use a pulling motion to 'sweep' him back to your side. In either case, continue to position him every time. You should demand precision work from your dog.

When your dog begins to anticipate your command, this is a good clue that he has learned what is desired of him. Continue training for a few more sessions. This will only build his confidence. After you are sure that your dog has a decent understanding of the sit, you should begin to use one command and instant slip chain correction. Give only one command; if your dog hesitates, then give an instant upward slip chain correction.

Each time you are successful in getting your dog to sit, give him a reward and praise as soon as his hind end is on the ground. Repetitions of this will enable him to learn what it is that you desire. Proficiency at the sit has been reached when your dog performs the action upon command with no hesitation and with no correction needed.

The Automatic Sit

Once your dog is proficient at the sit, then we can begin the process of teaching the automatic sit. The automatic sit is when the dog comes to a complete sit when the handler stops walking. This is a beneficial skill to have in a dog as it increases the dog's focus on the handler. This in turn invokes a sense of "wait for it" within the dog, which over time can result in the dog hanging on the handler's every move regardless of the distraction around.

The conditioning of the automatic sit is essentially the same as the standard sit except that this involves walking and coming to a stop. By this point it should take little correction to get your dog into a sit position, so the left hand applying pressure on the rear of the dog is not necessary. We will rely on the upward leash pressure alone to cue the dog that it's time to sit.

To begin this training you will start with your dog in a heel position. You will walk in a straight line for around ten or more paces at a normal walking speed. Slowly come to a stop, give the command "sit", and immediately apply the upward leash pressure. As soon as your dog has reached a complete sit, mark the behavior with "yes" and then reward him with his toy and praise. The command to sit should only be given during the first few times of conducting this exercise. After that, you should conduct the exercise using applied upward leash pressure only. You will walk in a straight line for around ten or more paces at a normal walking speed. Slowly come to a stop, applying the upward leash pressure. Again, As soon as your dog has reached a complete sit, mark the behavior with "yes" and then reward him with his toy and praise.

The end goal is to have your dog come to a complete sit every time that you come to a halt without having to command, cue, or correct him.

The Down

The next step will be training for the down position. Training the down position takes patience and persistence, as this position does not come easy for some dogs. Conditioning this behavior puts both the handler and dog into unusual positions within close proximity of one another. Therefore, it is important that you monitor the stress level of your dog while training this behavior. If you see that your dog is becoming increasingly agitated, stop the exercise. Conduct a simple obedience task that he is proficient at, and then reward and praise him. Take some time to play with him as this will help to calm any tensions within him before beginning again.

To begin, you will start with your dog seated in the heel position. Then you will kneel beside him. He should be on your left facing forward. Give the command "down". You will then put your left hand on the back of the dog, with your palm on the shoulder blades area. With this hand you will apply downward pressure which you will maintain throughout the down motion of the dog, until the final down position is reached. Next, you will take your right arm and slide it under your dog's chest area where you will grab your dog's left front leg with your right hand. In one motion you will apply downward pressure with your left hand while moving your right forearm forward in a motion parallel with the ground, sweeping both front legs out forward of the dog. This action should be conducted fluidly at a speed that is consistent but not so fast that it alarms the dog. The moment that your dog goes fully into the down position (front elbows completely on the ground), mark the behavior with a "yes" then reward and praise him. Your dog will most likely only remain down for a quick second so the timing of your reward and praise is of the utmost importance.

With the down position, as training progresses the method of reinforcement can progress as well. Once your dog begins to grasp the concept of the down position, you can transition away from sweeping the front leg, to just using slight down pressure on the shoulder area along with slight downward pressure with the leash. For this you will start with your dog in the heel position and give the down command. At the same time apply downward pressure to the shoulder blade area with your left hand. If your dog hesitates, give a downward correction with the leash by grabbing the leash near the clasp at the collar and giving a slight jerk toward the ground. Once your dog is down, reward and praise him.

K9 Ranger - Morehead City Police Department

When your dog has become proficient at the down, you can build speed by adding a toy into the equation prematurely. An exercise that I like to do is to place the toy on the ground in front of the dog a few feet away from him; I then give the down command. As soon as the dog goes into the down position, I release him to get the reward. This ensures timely reward and builds speed in dogs that are slow to go down.

The Stay

The stay is a key task that you should teach your dog to perform. This is especially the case with working dogs. There have been many times throughout my career as a police K9 handler where I have had to command my dog to stay in order to keep him safe. Such an instance would be if we were tracking a suspect and were coming up on a roadway to cross where traffic is flowing. I would command him to stay prior to him crossing the roadway so that we could wait for a break in traffic before starting the track again.

There are times where your dog may be unaware they are headed for dangers that they cannot see or do not understand. Being able to have your dog come to a halt upon command can be the difference in them remaining safe, becoming injured, or worse. You owe it to your dog to ensure that he is proficient at this task.

For service dogs such as medical or therapy dogs, the stay is equally as important. There will be a number of times in public when one would need to be able to place their dog into a stay position while they conduct a separate task such as paying for an item at the check out, or speaking with a person or group. There are even times when one would need for their dog to perform an extended stay which we will discuss later on.

In the beginning the stay command will be taught as a sit-stay, but the process for teaching the down-stay and the standing-stay is mostly the same. As you progress in your dog's training, you should include the stay command as a subsequent training lesson to each movement. As always, it is important to make sure that your dog is polished on each step before carrying on to the next.

To start training the stay you will begin with your dog in a seated heel position. While holding slight back pressure using the leash in your left hand, give the command "stay". With your right foot first, step out in front of your dog. The reason for stepping with your right foot first is based on the same understanding of non-verbal cues as we discussed with the moving heel. Stepping with your right foot first after giving the stay command will condition your dog to know that when you lead with your right foot, he is to remain in place.

If your dog breaks the stay as you begin to move away from him, give a firm "no" followed by a leash correction. Give the command once more to "stay" and repeat the exercise. Training this behavior may take lots of repeated practice. If you find that your dog is wanting to still move when you do, shorten the distance that you are attempting to put between him and you. Instead of attempting to step several steps away, only step a small step away and then quickly reward him for staying before he has the notion to move. This will help him better understand exactly what it is that you are wanting from him. Work this exercise until you are able to increase the distance to the point that you step out in front of your dog at the very end of your six foot leash.

Once the dog is steady on the stay, the stay time is extended and the handler's movements are broadened. You can accomplish this by walking around your dog after placing him in a stay position. Place your dog in a stay position, walk out to the end of your leash, and then begin to circle your dog counter clockwise until returning back to a heel position. Reward and praise your dog for the stay. When moving around him, be careful not to cause any sudden pressure or jerking with the leash, as this will likely cause him to move in the direction of the pressure. This type of exercise will aid in teaching your dog to remain in a stay even if you are moving continuously.

Once the stay is accomplished in the sit position, the same training can be conducted with your dog in the down position. It is important to initially train for the stay from a sit, as it is easier to make quick corrections when the dog breaks the stay position. When the dog is in the down position it is easier for the handler to find himself out of position to be able to make a correction in a timely manner.

The Recall

The recall, in my opinion, is the most important thing that you can train your dog to do. As discussed with the stay, the recall can also play a major role in the safety of your dog; not to mention reduce liability for you the handler as well. Being able to successfully recall your dog is the first step towards being able to work or enjoy your dog off leash.

Nowhere is it more imperative for a handler to have a solid recall with their dog than that of a law enforcement patrol dog team. The patrol dog is trained to do a number of tasks to include criminal apprehension. The handler for this type of dog must be able to send his dog to apprehend a suspect and have the ability to recall the dog from this task upon command. For this type of dog, the bite is one of the most satisfying events in the life of the dog. This is largely in part due to the amount of time dedicated to training for it and the manner in which it is trained. It is fun for the dog. So what does it take to achieve this level of training for your dog? What can make an animal avert from all instinct and primal nature only to return to the handler's side? The answer to this is twofold. It's an understanding of the dog's mind, and a commitment to the time and effort it takes to not only train for this, but to train to maintain it once it's achieved.

K9 Bolt - Saxonburg Police Department

Before we get into the *how* of training the recall, let's discuss the *why*, as in why would the dog want to come to you. What is it about you saying the word "here" that makes your dog choose to obey? Initially it will be the same as with any other command; conditioning. You will follow the steps of training, correct and reward appropriately, and eventually the dog will be conditioned to successfully complete the task at hand. But what happens when this is tested by a distraction? How do you as the handler remain more meaningful to your dog than any other outside factor? One word... fun. You have to be more fun to your dog than anything else. The word "here" has to become the word that lets your dog know that he is about to have that level of fun.

Throughout the training of this behavior your praise and reward for your dog should be over the top each and every time he returns to you. Think of your praise being an entire reward event in which you give lots of verbal praise accompanied with physical praise, and repeated play with the toy. It is your job to make sure that this training, as well as *all* training, is fun for your dog!

While the steps in this may sound simple enough to most, the technical workings lie within the actions of the handler as well as the continued training. It is important that you work to polish each portion of the actions on *your* part. Every move needs to be swift and smooth, and your timing of command and reward need to be on par. A dog, like a person, rarely gives more than what is asked of him. A dog that is asked to do something in a sloppy or carefree manner will inevitably perform what is asked of him with the same demeanor. This can result in an unfinished process where the dog appears to perform the task partially. One example of this I have seen in is where the handler attempts to call the dog to him, and the dog recalls to just out of the reach of the handler. Failure to correct this behavior will often lead to it becoming somewhat of a game for the dog. Especially if the handler lunges after the dog a time or two. To prevent this from becoming an issue we will give the dog the expectation of not only coming to proximity of the handler, but coming to a complete finished position. This will prevent there from being any time which would allow the dog to have mental lag where he could choose to do otherwise.

Before you attempt to condition this behavior you should first have a proficient sit and stay with your dog. To get started, place your dog in a seated stay and step out in front of him a leash-length away and turn to face him. When you turn and face your dog, leave your dog in a seated stay position for a few moments before giving the command for him to come. This will prevent the action of you turning and facing him from being perceived as a command to come to you. Once he has remained in place, give the command "here". As soon as the command is given, begin to 'reel in' your dog to you. Do not stop or pause until your dog is positioned in front of you. You should reel swiftly and smoothly enough to encourage a quick response to the command. Be careful not to reel so vigorously that it is perceived as a correction to your dog.

When your dog is in front of you, give the command for him to sit. If he fails to sit, give him a light upward correction to encourage him to sit. Even if he is proficient at the sit you should still use a light correction in this instance, as this may be the first time he has been instructed to sit in a position facing you. This could initially cause some nervousness for your dog. When he sits, reward and praise him immediately.

This exercise should be conducted multiple times a day. Regularly practicing these steps should result in your dog quickly progressing at the recall. Once he is consistent in being able to recall to a sit from a seated stay position, you should begin to practice recalling the dog from a moving position.

The first step in conducting this exercise is to place your dog on a 15 to 30 foot leash known as a 'long line'. This will allow you to test your dog's obedience to the command while ensuring that you have control enough to make him finish the task. Once on the long line, allow your dog to roam around. While your dog is roaming, call his name to gain his attention then immediately give the command. For instance you might say "Brutus, Here!" Then, in keeping with the initial exercise, you can begin to reel him in to you and have him come to a sit in front of you. When he goes into the sit position mark it with a "Yes" and then reward and praise him.

Take your time training this behavior. When you have reached a point where it is good… strive for better. Being able to recall your dog is a must-have prerequisite for upcoming off-leash training.

The Finish

The finish refers to the dog returning to the handler and coming to a seated heel position. This behavior is used extensively in competitive obedience, as well as most national, state, or local law enforcement canine certifying organizations. In those cases the dog will be instructed to perform a series of obedience tasks in which the dog will begin and finish in a seated heel position.

To train this behavior you should have your dog on a standard leash and place him in a sit position. Have him stay, and then step out in front of him a leash length away. Give the command "heel". When he begins to come to you, use the leash to guide him around behind you. As he is coming around behind you, take one step forward. When he gets fully around to your left side, take one step backwards and give the same upward leash pressure that you did for the automatic sit. Once he sits, reward and praise him.

These steps should be repeated multiple times throughout the training session. If you have taken time to properly condition each of the behaviors above, the finish should come fairly easy for your dog. Incorporate the finish throughout every obedience training session with your dog. The finish will give your dog a reference point for beginning and ending all training and exercises. You will become even more of a focal point for your dog, and his dependance on you for guidance will increase. This is also one of many tools that will work to strengthen the bond between you and your dog.

K9 Yuna - Carteret County Sheriff's Office

Chapter Five

Training Structure & Exercises

Once your dog is proficient at the individual behaviors discussed in the previous chapter, you should begin to combine them during single training sessions. In this chapter I want to go in depth with you on the structure of the training session itself. We will cover the time and duration of the training sessions, ways in which to combine tasks, and the overall structure of the training.

The methods and examples that will be discussed in this chapter (as well as the remainder of this book) have been used repeatedly throughout the years by staff at East Coast Canine to train successful law enforcement dogs across the nation. Anyone who has attended a law enforcement K9 handler school with us will tell you that obedience is something we take very seriously, and spend a lot of time focusing on. An obedient dog is a trusted dog.

East Coast Canine Basic K9 Handler Class 2024-1

What is Structured Obedience?

Let's begin with the definition itself. I define structured obedience as being the way in which the handler proposes to train certain behaviors in a particular manner, during a single session. It's the design of the training within the session itself. The job of the handler is to combine the training of behaviors in a way that neither overwhelms the dog or bores him to the point of uninterest. While the session can be formal or spontaneous, the training that is conducted within should be structured to best benefit the dog's progression of ability.

Formal Obedience Training

Formal obedience is obedience training that is conducted at a set time and location. It is best to conduct this type of scheduled training when you are conditioning a new behavior, or when problem solving any issues with your dog's obedience. The set time and location also gives way for you to improve upon your own dog handling skills such as leash handling, timing, etc. This is also a great time to begin introducing distractions in your obedience training. We will discuss distractions more in the coming chapters.

East Coast Canine Basic K9 Handler Class 2024-1

Spontaneous Obedience Training

Unlike its formal counterpart, spontaneous obedience occurs at random times and locations. For instance, you may be walking your dog from your car to your house and you have your dog sit, down, and then heel to the front door. Spontaneous obedience conducted regularly can be useful in building a quick response in your dog, as he will learn to obey commands and perform behaviors at any time and location.

K9 Apacs - Dunn Police Department

Benefits of Structure in Training

One of the most important foundations to have in dog training is structure. Training multiple behaviors at once sounds simple on the surface, however it should be done with the formality of a structure in order for you, the handler, to be able to properly monitor progress or regression within each behavior of your dog. Structure in training not only has a variety of benefits for the dog, but also for the handler as well.

One of the hurdles that we as dog trainers most often encounter is stress within the dog. A dog with a heightened level of stress can at times display a variety of different behaviors that indicate such. These behaviors (such as aggression, avoidance, or inattention) can negatively affect training. A trainer will have to spend time navigating these behaviors carefully in order to not further stress the dog, while also reaching the training goal. Structure within training is one of the methods that allows us to achieve this. Structured training can reduce the stress level for dogs; it creates a sense of familiarity for the dog. Even at times when the environment differs for your dog, the structure of the training that he is used to will provide him with a sense of familiarity and in turn lessen any anxiety that he may be feeling.

This benefits you, the handler, in many ways. Lessening the stress level of your dog can increase the success of training sessions. This will strengthen the bond between you and your dog. Dogs are pack animals and are always seeking to lead or to recognize the leader. The stability that you provide your dog in training will increase his trust for you. This all leads to one of the most important factors in your relationship with your dog: a stronger bond.

Equipment & Overview

For the exercises in this chapter you will use your standard six foot leash and have it attached to the live ring of your dog's slip chain collar. You will also need at least 4 small orange cones (the kind used in sporting events). Stake flags can be used in place of cones as well. The cones or flags will be used to mark the outlines for each exercise. This will enable the handler to have solid reference points for certain tasks.

As we continue to work our way through obedience training we will be using various structural outlines. These outlines for certain obedience tasks will be built upon as we move along. Eventually we will use these outlines to construct a full course for obedience training. The courses that we will be building will be modeled after those that are used by national and local canine certifying entities.

Exercise Principle

The exercises that we are about to employ will provide you with a blueprint for the type of structure in training that we have been discussing. The exercises will be broken down into three sections, and will cover every behavior that has been trained up to this point. The sections will be: heelwork, walking control, and distance control. The manner in which the behaviors are combined in these exercises closely resembles that of many national police canine certifying organizations. These exercises are part of our law enforcement canine course and certification at East Coast Canine Inc, and are the road maps in which we use to build and grow obedience in our dogs.

Each of these exercises should be trained in the order in which they are written in this book. At this stage in training each exercise should be trained with your dog **remaining on leash** throughout the duration of the training session. We will be discussing how to achieve off leash performance from your dog in the next chapter. Until then, remember to work all training at a pace that ensures your dog is getting thorough conditioning. Never do too much too soon.

Heelwork

For this exercise you will need an open area to train in. At this stage of training it is best to have an area that is free of distractions like a lot of people, vehicles, or other animals. This will ensure the best performance from your dog and allow you to accurately assess his progress.

To set this exercise up you will place one cone down and then walk out straight from it 30 paces and place another cone on the ground. Make a 90 degree turn to the right or left, walk an equal distance, and place another cone down. Repeat this process making the same direction turn and with equal paces between each cone until you have four cones on the ground in a square. The distance of 30 paces between each cone can be reduced as needed, so long as there is equal distance between each cone. I refer to this pattern as the "bracket" pattern obedience course. See the image below for reference.

Bracket Course

Once you have your cones or flags in place you will begin with your dog in a seated heel position at the start. Give the heel command and begin walking forward. When you get just past your first cone, make a right turn and continue straight. Make each turn a sharp 90 degree turn and give a slight jerk of the leash in that same direction. This will give a light activation of the slip chain collar letting your dog know that you are expecting an immediate turn. Make your next turn at the third cone in the same manner and continue walking straight. When you come to your fourth cone you are going to make a swift about turn. You are going to follow this pattern back in reverse making left turns on the way back. When you arrive back at the start/finish position, make a swift about turn, then come to a stop and finish position. Reward and play with your dog for his completion of the exercise. See the image below for reference.

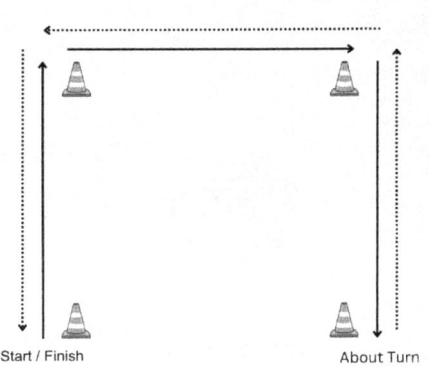

Bracket Course - Heelwork

An important thing to remember when conducting this exercise is to make each turn and about turn in a sharp manner, initially giving slight corrections at each turn and about turn. This will communicate to your dog that you are expecting the same level of sharp turns from him. Additionally, if your dog begins demonstrating behavior that suggests he is distracted such as nosing the ground, trying to walk away, or stopping, give the appropriate correction and get him back on task. Do not permit such behavior. Your dog should be focused on heeling beside you.

K9 Bolt - Saxonburg Police Department

Another variation of this exercise is one that I refer to as the "zig-zag" pattern obedience course. The cones again will be set between 20-30 paces at equal distances apart; however, this time they will follow a zig-zag pattern (hence the name). This pattern allows for the same number of turns and about turns as the first.

To set this exercise up you will place one cone down and then walk out straight from it 20-30 paces and place another cone on the ground. Make a 90 degree turn to the right, walk an equal distance, and place another cone down. You will then make another 90 degree turn back to the left, walk an equal distance, and place the last cone down. The distance of 30 paces between each cone can be reduced as needed so long as there is equal distance between each cone. See the image below for reference.

TRAINING STRUCTURE & EXERCISES

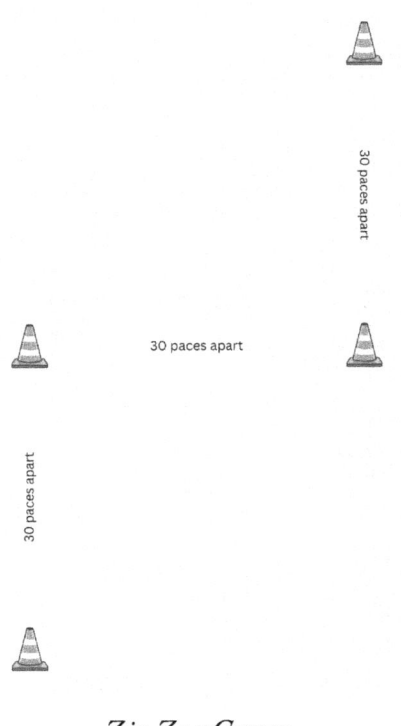

Zig-Zag Course

You will begin this course in the same manner that you did the bracket, at the start/finish with your dog in a seated heel position. Give the heel command and move forward following the cones as reference points to make your right and left turns. When you come to the last cone, conduct an about turn and complete the course in the opposite direction. When you arrive back at the start/finish position, conduct an about turn and come to a finish position. Reward and praise your dog.

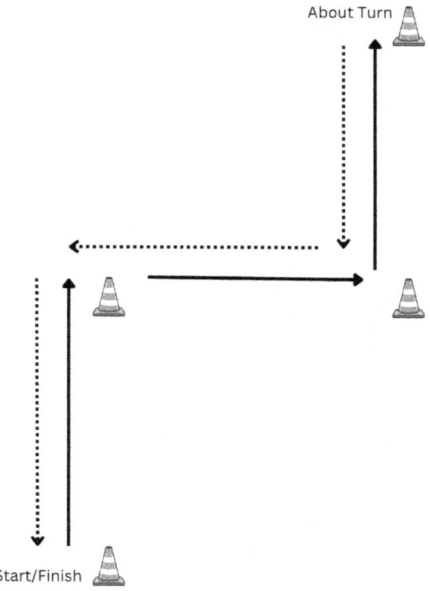

Zig-Zag Course - Heelwork

Walking Control

The next exercise that we are going to cover will be walking control. Walking control is essentially exactly what the name of the exercise implies: Control of your dog while he is in motion. If you're thinking that this sounds similar to heel work, you're partially correct. While it does involve heel work, the control part is focused on your dog performing obedience tasks during motion.

To set this exercise up you will use three cones. Place the first cone on the ground and then walk straight out from it about fifteen paces. There you will place the second cone on the ground and again walk straight out from it fifteen paces. Place the third cone down at this location. When you are finished you should have three cones in a straight line that are fifteen paces apart. See the image below for reference.

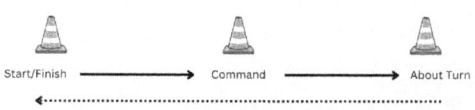

Walking Control

Before we start with the "how" of this exercise, let's discuss the end goal as well as the importance of this exercise. The goal is to be able to walk with your dog at a heel and give a command of either sit, down, or stay, and have your dog immediately perform that command while you remain walking in a forward motion away from him. This will eventually lead to you being able to continue walking away from him, conducting an about turn, and either walking past him, or having him return to a heel while you continue walking in a forward motion.

Why is this type of conditioning important for your dog to know? Conditioning your dog in this manner does several positive things for your dog's concentration and his overall ability to remain obedient to you. This will begin to shape your dog to depend less on the language of your body and more on the verbal cue given. It will also condition your dog to remain focused on you for direction, despite the changing image of the environment or location of his handler. Building your dog up in this manner will give him a firm foundation when it comes to introducing distractions in training. In the end, this will set him up for success when it comes to having your dog remain obedient in times when there are numerous distractions around. Now let's get started with the exercise.

K9 Bolt - Saxonburg Police Department

You will begin with your dog in a seated heel position standing to the left side of the first cone. Give the heel command and begin walking forward at a normal walking speed. When you reach the second cone, and without stopping your stride, give the command "sit". If your dog sits, continue walking until you reach the end of your leash. Remember, everything is on leash at this point so you will only reach the end of your leash, NOT the third cone. At the end of your leash conduct an about turn, walk back toward your dog, intending for your left side to be next to him. While continuing to walk, give the heel command along with a slight tug at the leash. He should snap right up into a moving heel with you. If so, continue back to the first cone and conduct an about turn coming to a finish. Reward and praise your dog.

Your dog initially may not comply with your command. Instead, he may attempt to continue to keep pace with you. Should this happen you should stop, give the command again and give the appropriate correction to go along with it. For example, let's say that you are walking and you give the command to sit and your dog keeps walking. At this moment you would stop, give the "sit" command once more along with a slight jerk upward on the leash. When your dog comes to a sit, you will continue to move forward. You may also have to follow these actions with the "stay" command prior to continuing to move.

Do not get discouraged if your dog does not immediately pick up on this exercise. Continue to work it in the described manner. Up until this point you have taught your dog to stick by your side, so this is all that he knows. This is the point in which you will begin to teach him to work independently of you. We want him working independently of you, however we also want him to remain obedient.

When your dog has demonstrated proficiency in completing this exercise with the sit, you will begin to incorporate the down command as well. You will begin with your dog in a seated heel position standing to the left side of the first cone. Give the heel command and begin walking forward at a normal walking speed.

When you reach the second cone, and without stopping your stride, give the command "down". If your dog downs appropriately, continue on with the remainder of the exercise. However, if your dog fails to down, follow through with the appropriate corrections for the down command, as mentioned in Chapter 4. Once in a down, give the stay command and continue on with the exercise.

Once you can successfully give ether command and have your dog remain in place while you walk to the end of your leash, conduct an about turn, and have him return to a walking heel, you are ready to attempt the pass by. To do this you will follow the same steps of walking, command, continuing to walk, and about turn. After the about turn you will approach your dog on your non-heeling (right) side this time. Here you will give the command "stay" as you continue to walk past him. When you pass him, you will continue walking until you reach the end of your leash where you will then conduct an about turn and re-approach him with him on your heeling (left) side. Give the command heel as you are continuing to walk.

It's important to mention here that dogs are really good at picking up non-verbal cues. Especially when those cues are associated with a command, and when the overall command/cue is repeated in training. One major tip I can give you for walking control training is to use your heeling side to re-approach your dog when you want your dog to begin heeling with you, and use your non-heeling side when you want to pass your dog and have him remain in place. For instance when you begin walking control you will be walking with your dog on your heeling (left) side. The command will be given to either sit or down. You will continue walking until reaching the point where you are to conduct an about turn. After conducting your about turn, if you wish to pass your dog by you will pass him by on your non-heeling (right) side.

Your dog will become conditioned to the cues of which side you pass on. Persistent training in this area will lead to your dog becoming so accustomed to your movements when approaching that you won't have to give a command for him to heel or stay as you approach. This conditioning is especially helpful for the transition to off-leash work.

In the chapter to come we will be adding additional movements and commands to this exercise. This is why it's important to take small steps here. This is the foundation that leads into being able to work completely off leash.

Distance Control

The name here suggests the action: Control of your dog at a distance. Up to this point we've established that control over your canine partner, whether a working dog or a pet dog, is an important goal to achieve. This would lead one to acknowledge that the next essential step to take in this journey with your partner would be to have that same control when he is away from you. Control of your dog from afar is not only key for mitigating liability; It is the ultimate sign of a strong relationship that has been formed through consistent training. When it comes to working dogs, distance control is the highest level of obedience that can be tested.

K9 Ranger - Morehead City Police Department

For this exercise we are going to follow the principle of start small, finish big. Initially you will begin conducting this exercise on leash using your standard six foot leash, and then transition later to your long line. This exercise will utilize the down, sit, and recall commands. This method is a good way to combine the training of all of these behaviors.

The use of multiple cones for this exercise will come later on in off leash training. For now you will use only one cone for this exercise. Place one cone down on the ground. This will be your reference point for conducting your distance control. This will be the location where your dog will be expected to remain. In a sense, this is the standard in which you will hold your dog throughout this training.

You will start with your dog in a seated heel position at the cone. Give the command "stay" and then step out in front of your dog remembering to step out with your right foot first. Once you reach the end of your six foot leash, conduct an about turn and face your dog.

If you have taken the time to properly train the stay position as discussed in Chapter Four, your dog should find this an easy task to obey. However, if your dog moves or breaks the stay then you should correct this behavior properly. Should your dog break the seated stay and attempt to walk toward you, give a firm "no" and take him back to the exact position that he was in next to the cone. It is important that you always bring your dog back to the position where you initially placed him in a stay. If your dog is breaking his stay he is doing so with the intent of closing the distance between him and you. Therefore, if he steps a few steps forward, and you allow him to remain at the location that he walked to, he has won. In his mind, he has achieved his goal of gaining ground. This will result in your dog continuing this behavior.

Once your dog is remaining in a seated stay position and you are at the end of your six foot leash facing him, you are ready to begin.

From this position give the command "down". When your dog goes into a down position upon command, allow him to remain there for a brief moment. Next, give the command "sit". When your dog goes into a sit position upon command, allow him to remain there for a brief moment. If your dog does not go into the sit or down when you give the command you should walk to him, repeat the command, and give the appropriate correction as we discussed in Chapter Four. Repeat the sit command once more. When your dog has returned to the final sit position, allow him to remain there for a brief moment. Next recall your dog back to a finish. Reward and play with him.

As your training in this exercise progresses, you can increase the number of 'reps' in the sit and down actions prior to the recall. If your dog is performing well, work on extending the time that you allow your dog to remain in each position. This will help to condition your dog to remain in a stay position for a longer period.

When your dog is proficient at this exercise on the six foot leash, you should then transition to the fifteen-foot long line. This is where you will begin to test your dog's ability to remain obedient at an extended distance. Don't rush moving to the fifteen-foot long line. The long line will offer little to no correction and will simply be used to maintain control of your dog from a distance, should he attempt to run off. The steps for conducting this exercise on the fifteen-foot long line are the same as before with the six-foot leash. Again, the important thing to remember is to bring your dog back to the place that you initially placed him, should he break from the stay position.

Introduction of Hand Signals

Hand signals are a great way to command your dog for many reasons. Hand signals can be useful when you are at a distance and need to place your dog into a sit, down, or even to recall your dog to you. They are exceptionally useful for the working dog, especially when remaining quiet or covert is of the utmost importance, or at times when you are around loud noises and your dog may be unable to clearly hear a voice command.

Training hand signals will follow the same principles of non-verbal cues that we discussed earlier in the walking control portion of this chapter. As mentioned, the conditioning will associate a non-verbal cue with a command, which will eventually lead to the dog understanding and complying with the non-verbal cue only.

It's not by accident that I choose to introduce hand signal training at the end of the distance control portion of this chapter. The exercise of training distance control provides us with the perfect outline for introducing and implementing hand signals.

If you have reached this portion of the book by way of your dog progressing along with the prescribed training, your dog should be proficient at the commands that we will be assigning hand signals to. Any command can be assigned a hand signal. However, for the purposes of this book we will be focusing on the basics of the sit, down, and stay. This will ensure that your dog is able to be controlled and restricted using hand signals only. You will learn the process of teaching and implementing hand signals with basic commands, which in turn will allow you to assign other hand signals later on as you choose.

The Down Hand Signal

To begin training a hand signal for the down position, begin with your dog on a standard six-foot leash, and place him in a seated heel position. Give the stay command and then step out in front of him. Transition your leash to your left hand. Raise your right hand straight up above your head. Give the command "down" and at the same time sweep your hand, palm down, in a downward motion in front of you, keeping your arm straight. Your dog should naturally follow the command and go down. When he does, toss him his toy reward, praise him and play with him for a moment. Repeat this process four to five times. After doing so, attempt to place your dog in the down position by using the described hand signal only.

K9 Ranger - Morehead City Police Department

The Sit Hand Signal

To begin training a hand signal for the sit position, begin with your dog on a standard six-foot leash. Place him in a down position, give the stay command, and step out in front of him. Transition your leash to your left hand. Next, you will give the command "sit". At the same time that you give the command, you will sweep your hand, palm up, in an upward motion in front of you. Your dog should naturally follow the command and come to a sit. When he does, toss him his toy reward, praise him and play with him for a moment. Repeat this process four to five times. After doing so, attempt to place your dog in the sit position by using the described hand signal only.

K9 Ranger - Morehead City Police Department

In the event that your dog fails to down or sit upon the display of the hand signal, you will need to give a correction so as to reinforce the command. Let's take a moment to discuss how to give a proper correction from this position. Being at the end of your leash can at times prevent you from being able to give a correction to your dog when needed. However, for training hand signals with distance control, there is an effective method.

Let's start with corrections for the down position. If you are at the end of your leash and have given the down hand signal but your dog has not complied, use the hand signal for down to give the leash correction. As you are coming down with your hand, allow your hand to hit the leash and press downward. Continue pressing down on the leash until your dog has reached the down position. Once your dog is in the down position, reward and praise him.

K9 Bolt - Saxonburg Police Department

Corrections for the sit position should be given in the same manner as with the down position, with the exception of the hand signal movement. If you have given the hand signal and your dog has not complied, use the hand signal for sit to give the leash correction. As you are coming up with your hand, allow your hand to hit the leash. Continue pressing up on the leash until you have fully brought your dog up into a sit position. When your dog is in the sit position, reward and praise him.

The Recall Hand Signal

The hand signal that I prefer to use for recalling my dog to a heel position is a tap of the left leg with my left hand. I find that the noise of the slap not only aids in getting the dog's attention but also gives a reference point for the dog to come to. To begin training a hand signal for recalling your dog, begin with your dog on a standard six-foot leash, and place him in a seated heel position. From here you will give the command "here". At the same time that you give the command, use your left hand to slap against the outer side of your left leg. When your dog arrives at this position and is seated, reward and praise him. Essentially this will become the hand signal that you will use to call your dog to a finish position.

The Stay Hand Signal

The stay hand signal will simply be placing your open hand straight out with your palm facing your dog. Think of a typical crossing guard stop motion. To begin training this hand signal, start with your dog in a seated heel next to you. Give the command "stay". At the same time you give the verbal command, give the hand signal. Next step off from your dog remembering to step with your right foot first. Then you will conduct an about turn and face him. From here throw him his toy and praise and play with him.

K9 Ranger - Morehead City Police Department

In training these hand signals, I strongly recommend using a combination or voice command and hand signal at the same time for each command. In the beginning stages use this combination so as to give clear instruction to your dog. The more you use the voice/hand combo, the more you set your dog up to successfully learn the hand signals. There is no set number of repetitions in training you can conduct that ensures your dog will adhere to the hand signal only. Conditioning your dog to hand signals takes time and patience. Consistency in training will ensure a steady progression in learning with your dog. As with all training, make it fun for them!

Chapter Six

Going Off-leash

A dog, while historically man's best friend, can be a companion of high liability. Every year reports are made of incidents involving dogs in which there is injury to persons or dogs. So much so that many insurance companies now offer dog liability insurance. While each incident has its own unique contributing factors, a number of these types of incidents can be prevented with smart handling and solid obedience training.

Whether you have a working dog or a pet dog, the most important level of training to achieve is control of your dog off-leash. Off-leash control is not just proof of a strong bond and conditioning, it's a level of training that is proven to lessen liability. Conditioning your dog to be obedient off-lead should be the goal of every canine handler.

In this chapter we will work to achieve this by following many of the same training exercises and principals that were set forth in the previous chapter. It is important for you to have read Chapter 5 prior to attempting the next level of training that will be discussed.

We will be using the exercises that were laid out in Chapter 5 as the framework for our transition to off-leash training. Therefore, it is imperative that you have a clear understanding of these exercises, and that your dog has a solid on-leash performance level before moving forward.

Patience is key, as there is no need to rush any level of dog training. Do not attempt too much too soon when it comes to off-leash obedience. Take your time throughout this chapter and really focus on polishing each step before taking the next one. Without a trainer present you will be the one who can determine when it is time to take the next steps with your dog. You will also be the one who has to make the call to back up a step with your dog when needed. A major key of off-leash training is knowing when to go back on-leash. Spend more than enough time on each step before moving on to the next. I can assure you, it will pay off dearly in the end.

Above all, remember... Like all other training, keep it fun for your dog!

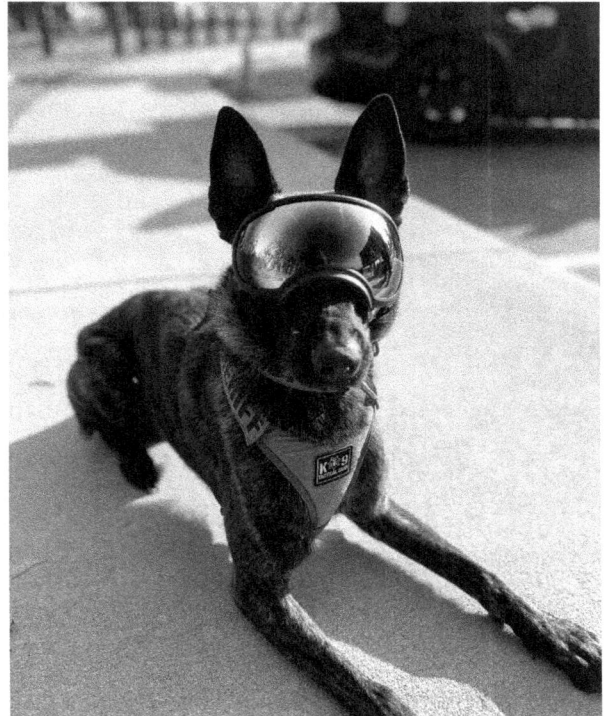
K9 Brutus - Currituck County Sheriff's Office

Off-Leash Heelwork

Off-leash heelwork will begin in the same manner as the heelwork portion of Chapter 5. Using your cones or flags, set up the bracket pattern obedience course. Start the course so that your first two turns will be right turns. Beginning with your dog in the seated heel position, run through the heelwork exercise with your dog on-leash, rewarding and praising him after completion. Do a couple rounds of this before moving on. At each turn, give a slight jerk of the leash toward the turn as you make it. This will serve to gently remind him to stick close with you at each turn, setting the tone of your expectations as we continue.

This should come easily to your dog at this point, enabling you to create a relaxed and fun environment for him. Reward and praise after each completion. Spend some time playing with him after each successful completion of the obedience course.

Next, reset to begin the course once more. With your dog on-leash and in the seated heel position, give the command "heel" and begin forward. As you begin to move forward drop your leash alongside your dog, allowing him to drag it along as he goes. A key point to remember is to not make an *event* out of dropping the leash. You should drop it smoothly without fumbling with it too much, and without breaking the cadence of your stride. You do not want to draw your dog's attention away from him correctly walking at a heel.

As you approach the first right turn, be sure to make the turn sharply just as you would if you were holding the leash. It is likely that your dog will turn with you and continue to follow. If so, continue on with the course with your dog dragging the leash. However, if your dog fails to make the turn with you, quickly recover your leash, give a slight correction, and get him back to a heel. Make the next right turn and give a sharp correction in the direction of the turn. Do not drop the leash again just yet. Make your about turn and give a correction here as well so that you can keep your dog moving sharply with you. After your about turn, drop the leash once more and continue moving forward with your dog at a heel. Approach the left turns with the same method as the rights; Follow through with corrections as necessary. As always, when you complete the course reward and praise your dog. Continue the training routine of conducting the bracket obedience course on-leash and then off-leash until your dog reaches the point where he is completing the course with little to no corrections in both scenarios.

K9 Bolt - Saxonburg Police Department

After some time of conducting the course in this manner you should attempt to complete the course beginning with your dog dragging the leash behind him and continuing to completion without you picking the leash up. Begin with your dog in the seated heel position. Without making it noticeable, drop your leash down by your side. Give the heel command and begin moving forward. Continue on with the completion of the course.

Dropping the leash does several things to help you work toward your dog being completely off-leash. It allows your dog to still feel some level of tension on his collar, making him believe that you still have some level of control of the leash. It also allows you to be able to stop him from straying away from you easily. You can do this by simply stepping on the leash. Many times, especially when making a right or left turn, or an about turn, you can give a slight correction by stepping on the leash momentarily. This will typically give a slight enough correction to remind your dog that he should be by your side and not straying away.

Once your dog has reached a point in his overall training that he can complete this course with the leash dragging, and with you having to give little to no correction, pick a day to attempt the course completely off-leash. When you arrive at your training location and set the course up, take your dog through the course on-leash, making it a point to conduct swift turns at each turning point. When you finish with one round of the course on-leash reward and play with your dog. After taking a moment to praise and play with your dog, return back to the seated heel position.

From this position, remove the leash completely from your dog. Be sure to do so without making it a big event. A good way to do this is to pet your dog and give a small amount of praise (not so much that you cause excitement) while removing the leash. Just gently drop the leash down by the side.

Once the leash is completely off, give the heel command and begin forward. The key here is to, as they say, *walk with a purpose.* Maintain the same integrity in your stride and approach as you would when your dog is on-leash. A tip I always use at this point in training is to maintain my same hand position as if I were still holding the leash. All of this combined will give the dog the illusion that you still have tangible control. Remember, you can still give a voice correction when necessary. Should your dog begin to stray, give a firm "no" followed by the heel command once more. Continue on with the obedience course making sure to create a big reward event for your dog when he successfully completes it off-leash. Give him his toy and lots of praise and play!

When you attempt this exercise completely off-leash, if you find that your dog is repeatedly attempting to stray from you, disobey the obedience commands, or any other form of disobedience, stop the exercise. Recall your dog back to you, hook him on-leash, and return to the start position. From here you will go back through the course on-leash completely. Along the way you should give slight jerks of the leash at every turn and about turn. When you complete the exercise you should still reward and praise your dog. Attempt the off-leash once more. If you find the same behavior occurring, your dog is not ready to proceed off-leash. Continue repeating the on-leash training procedures until proficiency is achieved.

At this point in training I'd like to take a moment to discuss a problem-solving tip. If at any point in the beginning stages of your off-leash training your dog decides to break away and frolic around, the worst thing you could do is chase after him. The moment that you chase and he moves away to just out of your reach is the moment that you introduce him to the game of keep away. Chasing after him while he is just out of reach will be an exciting event for him that he will continue to do. In this moment of defiance, instead of chasing after your dog, attempt to call him to you. If he fails to come, use the toy to get his attention. Do not throw it to him as this will only reward him for the bad behavior as well as leave you without a way to get him back to you. Instead, show the toy to him and wave it around. This should get his attention and he should come back to you. When he does, call him to a heel and secure your leash once more.

Once you have achieved a level of training where your dog has repeated success of off-leash completion of the bracket obedience course, switch it up to the zig-zag obedience course so as to provide a change of scenery and movement for your dog. Switch up working these courses. Work one during a training session and then use the other during the next training session. This will also aid in keeping your dog's attention and increase his focus on the training itself.

This stage of training has the potential to have hit or miss moments. Due to this, I recommend training in a location that is safe for your dog as well as safe for others. Pick a place that is secure should your dog break away from you. Fenced-in places provide a great location for this type of training. Baseball and football fields that are not in use are a solid option as well, provided that you can acquire permission to be there. During this stage of training your dog it is also a good idea to keep distractions to a minimum. The less we can tempt the dog to chase after something (such as a squirrel or jogger) while he is off-leash, the better chance we will have at properly conditioning his behavior.

As we continue through this chapter we will be discussing and employing various off leash exercises. Before continuing any further it is important that you take the time to ensure that your dog has achieved a solid workable level of off-leash heelwork. This will transpire through every other behavior that we will train for from here on out.

As I stress throughout this book, make this training fun for your dog! The more fun it is the more he will want to do it. For you the handler it is imperative that you closely monitor your frustration level. If you feel that you are getting frustrated during a training session, you should end that session. A frustrated handler will make poor decisions for his dog. Knowing when to end and when to begin could be the difference between failure and success.

Off-Leash Walking Control

Off-leash walking control will follow the same principle as off-leash heelwork in that you will conduct the exercise on leash initially and progress to dropping the leash while leaving it attached to your dog. Building upon this, you will again reach the point of being able to go completely off-leash. If you have truly taken the time to train for off-leash heelwork in the manner that was prescribed, moving to off-leash walking control should progress smoothly.

Begin by setting up the exercise using three cones or flags as described in Chapter 5. Initially you should conduct the training on-leash a couple of times. Reward and praise your dog upon each successful completion. After you complete a couple rounds of this exercise on-leash it will be time to drop the leash.

Standing to the left side of the first cone, place your dog in a seated heel position. Give the heel command and begin walking forward at a normal walking speed. When you reach the second cone, and without stopping your stride, give the command "sit". As your dog begins to sit, smoothly drop your leash and continue walking forward. When you reach the third cone, conduct an about turn and begin walking back toward your dog. As you approach him, make sure that he is more toward your left heeling side. While in motion, quickly retrieve his leash, give the heel command, and continue forward.

When you reach the first cone, conduct an about turn and continue toward the second cone. When you approach the second cone, give the command "down". As your dog begins to go down, smoothly drop your leash and continue walking forward. When you reach the third cone, conduct an about turn and begin walking back toward your dog. As you approach him, make sure that he is toward your left heeling side. While in motion, quickly retrieve his leash, give the heel command, and continue forward. When you reach the first cone, conduct an about turn and come to a finish position. Reward your dog with his toy and lots of praise.

Once your training has reached the point where your dog is performing proficiently at this level, you will be ready to drop the leash completely. For this you will follow the same procedures for dropping the leash as mentioned above in the Off-Leash Heelwork portion of this chapter.

Begin the exercise as normal with the leash in hand. Give the heel command and begin moving toward the second cone. At the second cone give the sit or down command. The moment your dog begins to move into position you will smoothly drop the leash. This should be done in one fluid motion while you are still in motion forward. When you reach the third cone, conduct an about turn and re-approach your dog on the heeling side. As you begin to come beside him, give the heel command. Do not pick up the leash. From this point forward during the exercise your dog will drag the leash beside him.

Continue walking with your dog at a heel until you reach the first cone. Conduct another about turn. If your dog does not turn immediately with you, simply step on the leash. This will cause a light correction to be given should he continue forward. Once he begins to turn with you, step off the leash and continue walking with him at a heel. When you approach the second cone, give the sit or down command. When you reach the third cone, conduct an about turn and walk back to your dog picking them up at a heel again continuing forward to the first cone.

When you arrive at the first cone this time you will conduct an about turn and halt. What you want to see from your dog here is him following the about turn with you, and stopping and sitting when you come to a halt. Should he not do this, recover your leash and then conduct a few repetitions of about turns where you halt and place him into a sit. Do this with the appropriate corrections until he seems to understand exactly what you desire from him.

Once you can successfully give either command and have your dog remain in place while you walk to the next cone, conduct an about turn, and have him return to a walking heel or a finish position, you are ready to attempt the pass by. To do this you will follow the same steps of walking, command, continuing to walk, and about turn. After the about turn you will approach your dog on your non-heeling side. Here you will give the command "stay" as you continue to walk past him. When you pass him, you will continue walking until you reach the next cone where you will then conduct an about turn and re-approach him with him on your heeling side. Give the command heel as you are continuing to walk. From here you can continue on with the exercise, switching from passing your dog by to picking him up at a heel at re-approach.

Continue conducting the above mentioned walking control exercises for several training sessions, allowing your dog to drag the leash. When has reached a point of being able to successfully complete the exercises and follow you, and you feel confident that he will remain obedient, you can attempt to conduct walking control off-leash completely. To do this, allow your dog to remain on-leash until you are at the starting point and he is in a finish position. Remove the leash in a casual manner so as not to alert your dog. From this position you will conduct the exercise normally. If your dog starts to stray away or not remain in place, give verbal corrections and commands to get him back where he needs to be. Should you find yourself having to do this often, stop the exercise, place him back on-leash and conduct the exercise multiple times giving appropriate corrections as needed.

Remember to praise, reward, and play with your dog excessively after each successful completion of the exercise whether on or off-leash.

K9 Bolt - Saxonburg Police Department

Off-Leash Distance Control

First and foremost, I will be honest here. This is often the point that proves to be the most frustrating when it comes to dog training. Training a dog to be completely obedient when he is free from any physical connection to his handler can be a tedious task that requires the utmost patience. Before we get into the *how* of training for distance control I want to discuss some of the issues that you may immediately be up against when it comes to training this behavior.

Owning or working a dog creates a serious bond between dog and handler. So much so that at times it can cause your partner to not want to be away from you. This doesn't just apply when you leave them at home when you head off to work. This can even be the case when you are just a few feet away from them. In the canine training world we refer to this as separation anxiety. Meaning that your dog does not want to be away from you either by distance or time.

Dogs can display a number of different behaviors when it comes to separation anxiety. If you are within sight of them it will typically make them want to be near you to the point they will not leave your side even when commanded, or tempted with play. At times when you are out of sight it could cause your dog to act more aggressive than normal which may appear in the form of constant barking or chewing at items within their reach. Generally speaking, the root cause of this is tension. Tension causes a dog to not think clearly, and above all, during training we want a clear-thinking dog.

As we move through training for this behavior I will discuss some practical methods for dealing with any symptoms of the above mentioned issue that may arise. Following this instruction closely and remembering not to attempt too much too soon, will greatly aid in your success at training your dog to be obedient at a distance. Now for the *how* of distance control training.

The first step in this process is to not immediately go off-leash. Take a few moments to get your dog 'into the groove'. Use the on-leash method of distance control training that you have been doing up to this point as a way to get him warmed up to the exercise. Conduct a few repetitions prior to leaving the leash behind. I strongly recommend that at this point in the training you give all verbal commands in conjunction with the corresponding hand signal. This gives your dog a physical cue to focus on when at a distance, and will reassure him of the command in which you are given. This is also a great pathway to successfully being able to command by hand signal only. As always, throughout this training remember to reward and praise him upon each completion. This will ensure his attention will remain on you and the task at hand. In turn, this will also aid in mitigating any issues of separation anxiety.

Once you have completed a few rounds of this exercise on leash, you will transition into training with the leash out of your hand but still attached to your dog. The best way to do this discretely is do it immediately after placing him in the seated stay position, and just before you would walk out to what would be the end of your leash. With your dog seated, give him the verbal command to stay, along with the hand signal for stay. At this point you will casually drop the leash. From here you should walk out to the normal leash-length distance away from your dog. Next, you will give the down command along with the hand signal for down. When he goes down, throw the toy to him and praise and play with him a lot!

Let me take a moment here to explain the reward process for distance training. It is important to throw the reward to him just prior to beginning to praise him. We want to focus on the distance, and rewarding him for actions at that distance. Throwing the toy allows him to remain at that distance in order to receive the reward. If you begin to praise first and he breaks position to come forward and receive the toy, you will in turn teach him that he can achieve the toy by moving toward you. This will only further increase tension within your dog. His anxiety will increase the longer he is at the distance because he will only be focusing on how to get to you for the toy. This is eliminated when he begins to expect the toy to arrive at exactly where he is at.

From here you will repeat the same steps of placing your dog in a seated stay, dropping the leash, and walking a leash-length away. You will again give the down command only when your dog goes into a down position, this time allowing him to remain there for a couple of seconds. Now give him the sit command along with the sit hand signal. When your dog comes to a sit, again throw the toy to him and begin to praise and play with him.

Continue with this training exercise and slightly increase the distance each session. A good initial goal is to be able to place your dog in a sit and a down while having him remain at a distance of approximately ten paces away from you. This may take as few as a couple training sessions, or as many as a few weeks of regular training. As I have stressed throughout this book so far, patience is key here. Once this level of training is achieved you will be ready to go completely off-leash.

When it comes to removing the leash completely, follow the exact same steps previously mentioned for dropping the leash. Place your dog in a seated stay and casually remove the leash. This can be done while petting him with one hand and gently unhooking the leash from the collar with the other hand. Once the leash is removed, reinforce the stay by giving the command and hand signal once more. Walk about a leash-length distance away. Start from this position again, because up to this point he will be most accustomed to you being the leash-length away. From here, continue to follow the above steps in increasing the distance with each session. Always throw the toy to your dog, remembering to praise and play once your dog has acquired the toy.

If at any point in your progression through this training you find that your dog is breaking the position either by completely abandoning the position and coming to you, or by creeping forward during the sitting or downing action, it's a good indicator that it is time to go back on-leash. Going back on-leash will afford you the opportunity to use proper corrections to aid in shaping the desired behavior from your dog. This will be the same corrections that you learned during the initial on-lead training for the commands. If your dog breaks the sit, return him to the position and correct in the manner that invokes a sit with your dog. If your dog creeps forward when downing, return your dog to the position, give the down command and correct downward.

Keep training sessions for distance control relatively short. This can be stressful conditioning for your dog. Overwhelming him can cause setbacks that will result in your dog developing unwanted behavior. If at any time during a training session you see that your dog is becoming too stressed, stop the distance training by returning your dog on-leash, giving a simple command such as 'sit', and then reward and praise him greatly. Spend time playing with him by tugging or playing fetch. Create a big reward event and turn it into play time before ending the session.

K9 Bolt - Saxonburg Police Department

Continuing Off-Leash Training

One of the most important things to know when it comes to off-leash training is knowing when to go back on-leash. It's good practice to go back on-leash at times when you find your dog distracted or disobedient during your training session. If you find that your dog's performance is 'slipping' during a training session, stop the exercise, secure your dog back on-leash, and begin the exercise once more giving the appropriate corrections as needed.

Another good practice of going back on-leash occurs at the beginning of the training session. Conduct the training exercise on-leash at least once before removing the leash. This applies even when your dog is proficient at the off-leash exercise that you are going to be training. Doing this will help to keep your dog sharp and aid in increasing his reaction time to your commands.

When it comes to your dog's off-leash obedience skills, it is imperative to conduct training regularly. The more often you train with your dog, the better his skills will become and remain. As mentioned earlier in the book, begin and end each session on a positive note!

K9 Ares - Jackson County Sheriff's Office

Chapter Seven

Putting it All Together

Throughout the book so far, our training has focused on conditioning your dog to complete individual tasks. Now we will aim to take all that you and your dog have learned up to this point and put it together into a single training session. We will do so through the use of training courses for your dog. These training courses will include all of the obedience commands that your dog has learned so far. This training will be structured in a way that will allow you to train your dog in an overall 'big picture' manner while also providing you the ability to *zoom in* and see areas that your dog may need extra training on. The goal is to continuously and consistently train all obedience behaviors. While the training session will have structure, it is able to be modified to meet the needs of your dog.

Benefits of Using a Training Course

Think of a training course as a full body workout. Let's say you find an hour in your day to exercise and choose to complete a full body workout at your local gym. You start with the upper body and progress until finishing the workout off with lower body. You successfully complete bench pressing, curls, pull-ups, sit-ups, deadlifts, squats, and leg extensions. However, during this workout you find that you struggled a bit with pull-ups. You weren't able to do as many as you had intended to do and your form got sloppy halfway through the exercise. Instead of continuing everyday with the same workout, you take this information and use it to your advantage. At the next gym visit you incorporate more pull-up activities into your workout and use additional training aids to help you build your skill and abilities in this area. And after doing so, you find that your training has paid off and your pull-up skills are now on par with the rest of your workout.

Your goal should be to do the same with your dog's skills. You as the handler should always be working to train your dog to become better and better. The best tool that you have for doing this is conducting training that provides a way to highlight the good, as well as the not-so-good behaviors. Doing this provides you, the handler, with two very effective benefits.

In highlighting the good behaviors, you are able to see the fruit of your labor. You get to see all of the time and hard work that you have put into training your dog finally pay off. If your dog is coming to a firm and aligned finish position right beside you every time you call him to a heel, you can know for a fact your training is paying off. You will think back to the many hours that you have spent conditioning your dog for this behavior. Not only will this give you a great sense of accomplishment, but it will also give you the motivation to further your training. You can know from this fact that you will be able to sharpen the other behaviors of your dog by applying the same time and consistency into training. When these moments happen, don't let them pass by quickly. Take the time to admire your accomplishment as a handler, and most importantly, take the time to allow your dog to admire it. Play with him, praise him, and reward him at the highest of levels to ensure that he knows what a good dog you think he is!

On the opposite end of the spectrum, highlighting the not so good behaviors allows you to know exactly what it is that you need to focus your training on. This will provide a map for you to follow allowing you to remain consistent in your training. If your dog shows deficiency in an area, don't get frustrated and don't give up. Instead, use this as a focus point for your upcoming training. Remain focused on this deficiency in training until your dog has reached the desired level of proficiency. Many times I have seen handlers avoid a particular task with their dog simply because it frustrates them that their dog will not perform the task to a level of their liking. This only makes the deficiency worse as the dog is getting little to no training on the issue and only inconsistent training at best. For example, should your dog develop an issue with distance control, it will be counterproductive for you to exclude distance control from your training session. What you should be doing is incorporating *more* distance control training into your session, using the tools and tactics that you've learned to correct the issue. Keep in mind, as always, that consistency is key.

Building the Course

When it comes to the layout and content of these training courses all should be familiar. Throughout this book we have taken the course as a whole and broken it down to its finest points. We have taken that and in turn used it as the foundation of which the entire obedience instruction has been built. This enables us to make a seamless transition as we now put it all back together.

The first step in this 'reconstruction' will be building the course itself. Which again, should be familiar as we will be working with the bracket-style and zig-zag style courses that have been previously discussed. The only addition that we will be making to the set ups themselves is the addition of another cone.

The additional cone will be placed on the first leg of each style course at a distance of halfway in between the first and second cones. This will be the mark for your walking control commands as well as your dog's position for your distance control portion. **View the "Course Examples" section of this chapter in order to see how each course should be set up.**

Initially, I prefer to start training dogs with the bracket-style course. This is mostly due to the same direction turns being repeated. This allows me to focus on the sharpness of the turn with the dog. For instance, if I have to give a correction at the first right turn, I have another right turn immediately coming up that I can use to judge the effectiveness of the correction given. Once the dog becomes familiar with the routine of the bracket style course, I will periodically switch to the zig-zag style course to change up the pattern for him. This works to keep your dog on his toes, requiring him to remain attentive.

As you progress in your training you can use these courses interchangeably, as you see fit, to get the best results from your dog. **For consistency and ease of understanding, throughout the remainder of this chapter I will be referring to the bracket-style course for instruction.**

Course Example - Layout

Bracket

PUTTING IT ALL TOGETHER

30 paces apart

   30 paces apart

 15 paces apart

 15 paces apart

Zig-Zag

Training Session Length

Using the course, the training session will flow in the same order that you have progressed through obedience training up to this point. You will begin with heelwork. Once heelwork is completed you will then move on to walking control, and then finally distance control.

For each training session a good rule of thumb is to only complete the entirety of the course no more than three times. This is to ensure your dog is not getting bored or overworked, which would result in an unsuccessful training session. Course completions can vary depending on the amount of time you have available for training. For instance, if you have fifteen minutes to spare for a quick session then I would recommend conducting the course once, following immediately with any remedial training needed, and then spending the remainder of the time playing with your dog, so as to suffice the rule of ending all training on a good note. Should you have an unlimited amount of time then I would spend around a half hour, give or take, on the training session in whole. This would allow you the necessary time to complete the course in its entirety two to three times with adequate corrections, rewarding, remedial training, and play included. By no means should training be limited to a half hour per day. You may have more than one training session using the courses per day. It is best practice, however, to limit each training session itself to around that time frame.

By now you should be comfortable and confident in conducting heelwork, walking control, and distance control with your dog. You should have a good understanding of how and when to give corrections, as well as praise in order to shape and condition your dog's behavior. In an effort to not oversaturate this book with repetitive language, I will not write a step by step procedure for conducting each exercise. Please revisit Chapter 5 any time you would like a refresher on the procedures themselves. However, I will explain the process for working through the course properly to include the most effective way of rewarding. I will also explain the best way to use the courses to remediate any deficiencies your dog may have.

Working Through the Course

Once you have set up the bracket course, you are ready for the training session. Throughout the course, you will begin and end each exercise at the start/finish cone with your dog in a finish position. You will reward and praise your dog at the end of each exercise when he has returned to a finish position at the start/finish cone. After rewarding your dog, place him back into a finish position, pausing for a moment to refocus his attention, and then begin the next exercise.

The course should be viewed as three separate sections that flow together:

1.) Start/Finish Position
   - Heelwork

   - Return to Start/Finish Position

   - Reward

2.) Start/Finish Position
   - Walking Control

   - Return to Start/Finish Position

   - Reward

3.) Start/Finish Position
   - Distance Control

   - Return to Start/Finish Position

   - Final Reward + Play

At the end of your final exercise your reward should become a short play session with your dog. This will allow him to relax from any tension that he gained throughout the training session as well as increase the bond between you and him. Take a moment to view the course examples on the following pages. This will provide you with a visual example of how to properly conduct each portion of the course.

Course Examples - Heelwork

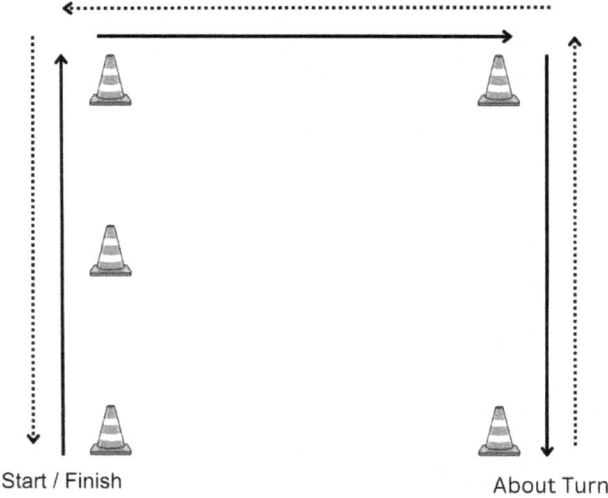

Bracket - Heelwork

PUTTING IT ALL TOGETHER

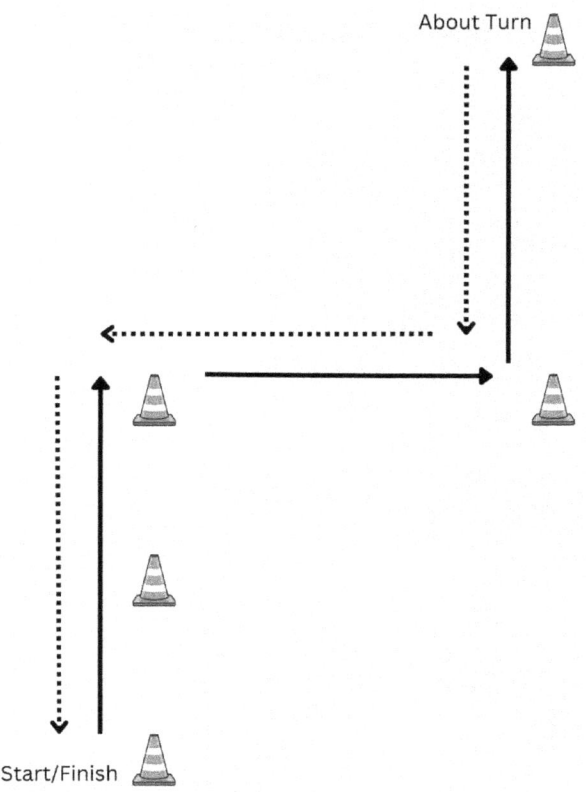

Zig-Zag - Heelwork

Course Examples - Walking Control

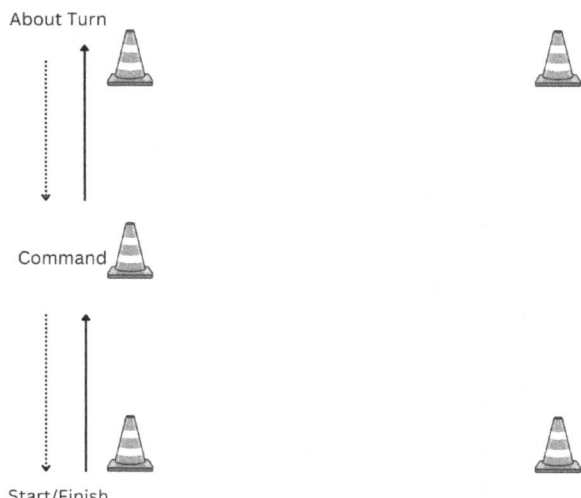

Bracket - Walking Control

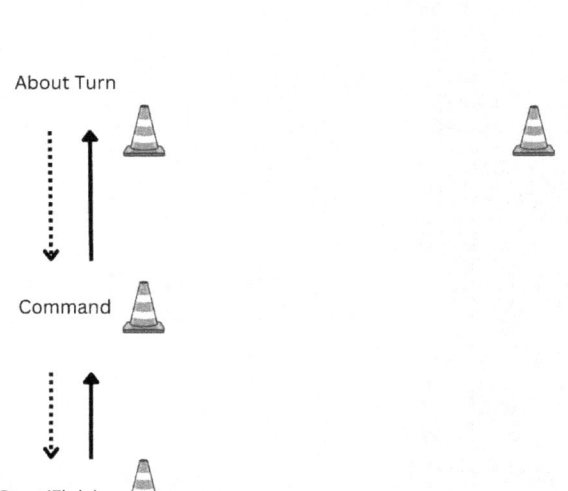

Zig-Zag - Walking Control

Course Examples - Distance Control

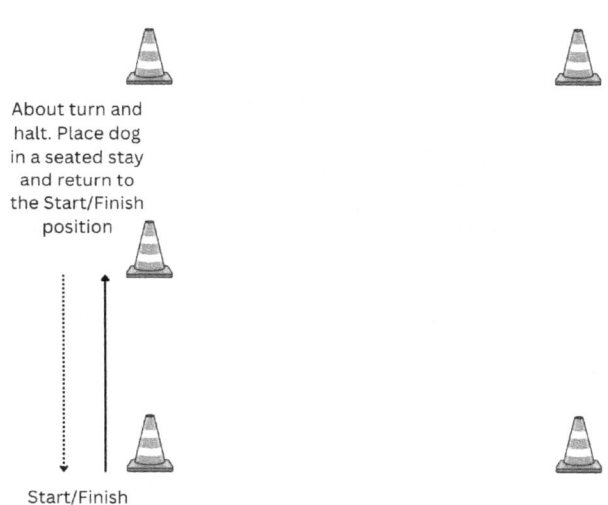

Bracket - Distance Control

PUTTING IT ALL TOGETHER

About turn and
halt. Place dog
in a seated stay
and return to
the Start/Finish
position

Start/Finish

Zig-Zag - Distance Control

Chapter Eight

Advanced Theory & Practices

In this chapter we will be further discussing theory and practices that will carry your dog training to the next level. Taking the time to further understand your dog, and implementing practices that proactively stimulate your dog's mind, will work in your favor when it comes to training.

Spontaneous Rewarding

We all desire to have an obedient dog that is incredibly attentive and responds quickly to our every command. It's true that this can only be achieved with regular consistent training. However, there is one simple element you can add to your training that can very quickly begin producing these desired actions within your dog.

Take a moment to reminisce with me. You're in 10th grade, last period (for me, it was unfortunately algebra), and it's Friday at 2:30. Your teacher is still lecturing but all you can think about is hearing the bell ring signaling your escape into weekend bliss. The longer the teacher talks, the more often you glance at the clock. As the second hand glides past each mark you become more and more impatient. You feel your leg start to bounce up and down rapidly. You're fumbling your pencil around in your hands. Your attention is anywhere else but on what the teacher is saying. Finally the bell alarms. Unknowingly you instantly feel the release of a dopamine rush as you jump to gather your things and escape to freedom. As you pass through the door your attention returns to the present allowing you to regain focus on the world around you once more.

The attention span of humans can vary from person to person. In the same manner they can vary from dog to dog. Certain factors such as breed, age, training level, etc can affect the attention of dogs. According to most Veterinarians, the attention span of dogs can range from 2 seconds up to 27 seconds for a single thought.

How does understanding the attention span of your dog help you with training? For starters, it can help shape your expectations for your dog. As a dog owner, it is easy to desire extremely high performance from your dog daily and to demand even more from your dog during your training sessions. If you are a working dog handler, your training sessions must come with a high level of demand especially when preparing for obtaining certifications. Additionally, understanding the dog's attention span can allow you to understand just how powerful rewarding our dog truly is. Everything you experienced when the bell rang on a Friday when you were in school is likely equal to the same release of tension your dog experiences when you throw him the toy after he's been obedient to your every command. Understanding this, we can easily see how rewarding the dog more often would be beneficial; however, let's not stop there.

Let's go back once more... 10th grade, Friday at 2:30, teacher lecturing. Only this time your teacher is throwing out pieces of candy for every correct answer that is given. Your attention is now somehow amazingly able to remain on your teacher. Yes the bell is soon approaching, however, you don't want to miss the opportunity to solve for *y* and have a mini Snickers bar launched across the room in your direction.

What you now see in this equation (pun intended) would be an example of a spontaneous reward. When it comes to training your dog, rewarding spontaneously can be instrumental in shaping your dog's behavior. Spontaneous rewarding during training can lengthen your dog's attention span and work wonders for keeping his focus on you and the task at hand. Let's discuss what exactly this looks like.

Take for example obedience training. You may typically train heelwork, sit, down, and stay all in one training session, which is common practice for most handlers. The majority of handlers will begin with their dog in a seated heel position, conduct heelwork with multiple turns in both directions, stop to do sit and down commands, maybe integrate some distance control training, return to heelwork, then finally come to a finish where they then reward and praise their dog. Again, very common practice.

Training for a lengthy duration without reward can at times produce unwanted behaviors from your dog. Such behaviors such as nosing the grass during heelwork or breaking the stay during distance control training, etc. are often the result of boredom or anxiety. Both of which from my experience can be mitigated with proper rewarding of the dog. So just what does this look like?

Take the normal training session, as described above, and sprinkle in moments of rewarding throughout. You would begin your training with heelwork and while walking in stride with your dog you would randomly drop the toy in front of them and begin praising and playing with your dog. This may happen after 30 paces or within the first 5 paces. During the sit and down drills you would give the sit or down command and then immediately give the toy and praise to them upon them performing the requested action. Sometimes it would be after the first sit or down action or maybe after two or three command and action instances. For the distance control parts you would give the sit or down command and when the dog performed it you would randomly throw the toy to them and begin praising and playing with them. Instead of completing all the commands and then calling them to a finish for their reward every single time, you will be integrating the reward as a part of the training as a whole.

Conducting training sessions in this manner will condition your dog to be readily focused on you. Your dog will think "I know this guy has my toy, I don't know exactly when I will get it but I know it can come at any moment so I need to stick with him closely and follow every command." Without going into the psychology of it all this is essentially the same characteristics that slot machines have on humans. It's not the reward itself but rather the desire for the reward that keeps you focused and coming back for more. Same as with your canine partner.

Don't be stingy with the reward. Training has to be fun for your dog and fun comes in the form of reward and praise for them. Driving them harder to achieve that reward doesn't always bring about positive behavior conditioning. Throw the candy, ring the bell, and give them their weekend just as often as your 10th grade self would have wanted it.

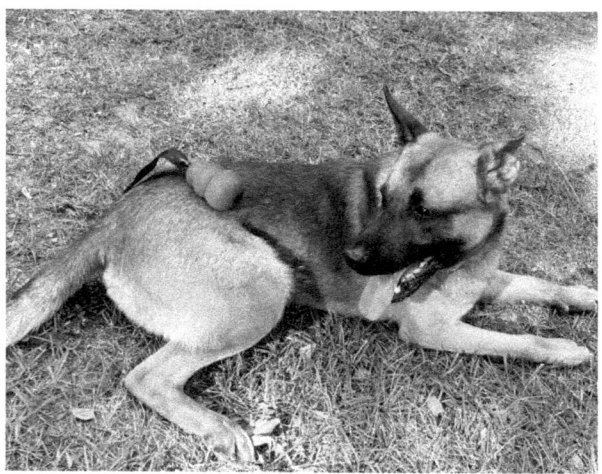

K9 Boone - Rocky Mount Police Department

Dopamine and the Variable Reward

Let's talk for a moment about dopamine. Dopamine is a neurotransmitter that relays information between neurons and special target cells throughout the body. It is responsible for many things within the body such as sleeping, mood, attention, motivation, and even muscle movement. Most notably, dopamine is responsible for triggering the feeling of wellbeing. All of the same is true for the mind of the dog.

When released, dopamine causes a sense of "feel good." It's that little rush of excitement you get when you pull in the driveway and see that your Amazon package is sitting by the front door. While dopamine has historically been linked to reward, recent studies have concluded that the dopamine release is more about the seeking than the actual receiving of the reward. There is a higher release of dopamine while searching Amazon for your perfect item than there is in actually receiving it. It's the *thrill of the hunt*, so to speak. The thought of "maybe there's a better deal to be found on the next page" fuels the feeling associated with the search. Interestingly enough, this is the brain response that occurs when you play a slot machine or use social media. Both of which have been strategically designed to create this response within you. Why? Because it means you will want to come back again and more often.

By now I am sure you're wondering just how this crash course in brain chemistry fits into a book about dog training. The more we can understand about the dog's responses to our actions, the better we can understand how to propose our actions towards the dog in order to achieve the desired action from the dog. To begin to tie all of this together, we must now discuss the variable reward.

In the 1950's an American psychologist and behaviorist B.F. Skinner conducted a series of controlled tests in which lab mice were kept in a box where they could press a leaver and receive a treat. The mice initially learned to press the lever by being allowed to roam freely around the box where they would eventually accidentally bump into the lever, in which a treat would be released. In no time the mice learned to press the lever to receive a treat. Skinner took this research a step further by splitting the group of mice up into two different boxes. In one box, when the mice would press the lever they would receive the same sized treat each time. In another box, the mice would press the lever and sometimes receive a large treat, a small treat, or no treat at all. Skinner observed that the mice who received varying rewards became nearly obsessive over pressing the lever in comparison to mice who received the same reward every time. This is in direct correlation to the dopamine that was released during the seeking of the reward. Those mice received an increased dopamine release at the press of the leaver, whether there was a large treat, small treat, or even when there was no treat at all.

All of this allows us to know that when training our dog, if we vary the reward, we can increase the anticipation for the reward. If we can increase the anticipation for the reward then we can increase the focus on the action that triggers the reward. In turn, the desired behavior becomes reinforced, resulting in a quicker and stronger response from your dog. Conditioned behavior replaces instinctive behavior to improve the probability of success for your dog.

> **Anticipation + Reward = Reinforcement**

K9 Kadjar - Currituck County Sheriff's Office

Dog Decisions

As you move along on the journey of training your dog, there is one thing to keep in mind. There is no such thing as 100% reliable dog training. At the end of the day your dog is a dog. By that I mean that there will always be times, no matter how well trained a dog is, that he will absolutely just be... a dog.

Oftentimes when the dog is presented with an opportunity to make a trained decision or what I refer to as a 'dog decision', instinct will drive him to make the dog decision. For instance, if you have placed your dog into a stay position and then a squirrel runs across in front of him, there is a high probability that instinct will kick in causing your dog to make the dog decision to chase after the squirrel. You could get a similar reaction from your dog due to a number of different things such as a passing jogger, a cyclist, or another dog being present. You won't immediately know what things or objects may cause your dog to revert back to instinctual behavior, only time and exposure will reveal this. When you notice that something triggers this in your dog, make a mental note of it so that later on you can begin conditioning him for that particular situation.

It's not only carnal instincts that can be the cause of dog decisions. In the same way that we as people have bad days, dogs can have bad days too. Like us, dogs can be tired, fatigued, sick, or irritable. Any of which can be the driving force behind a particular action that they are taking or not taking. Simply put, despite any level of training, sometimes your dog will have an off day. When this happens, take it easy on your dog for the day. If you experience this during a training session, end the session and go back to things that are bond building activities like playing with him using his favorite toy.

While it is impossible to train a dog to refrain from his carnal desires or to teach the dog not to have a bad day, we *can* train to manage the behaviors associated with those things. A solid foundation of obedience training will greatly increase the chance of your dog's success.

Introducing Distractions

In any kind of training, human or canine, to achieve the best outcome you have to train for the scenario itself. This is where training with distractions comes into play. Training with and around distractions is key in building your dog's confidence in your leadership.

The first thing you should know and adhere to is that you should never add distractions to training unless your dog is already proficient at the behavior that you are asking of him. For instance, if you are still training your dog on how to stay, you shouldn't take him to a busy park and conduct a training session for this. The result will be an unfair amount of corrections to your dog with the training session ending in frustration for the both of you. Instead, you would work with him one on one until he is able to remain at a stay successfully. From there you would slowly introduce distractions for him to work through. This way he has a clear understanding of what you are asking of him. Remember, we always want a clear-thinking dog. When a distraction comes into the picture it elevates your dog's heart rate and thought processing, and lowers his ability to focus. Starting with too high of a level of distraction, or too many distractions, can overstimulate your dog causing failure in the training session overall.

K9 Ranger - Morehead City Police Department

The best practice for introducing distractions in the training session is to begin with one isolated distraction and work from there. What I have found to be the best initial distraction to use is the dog's reward toy.

To begin introducing the toy as a distraction simply place it on the ground out in front of your dog. Do this while your dog is in a finish position next to you. Your dog may initially attempt to break his stay and make a dash for the toy. If this happens, catch him before he gets the toy. Give the appropriate correction, command him to sit and stay. Once he does this, tell him "free" and allow him to get the toy. Take a moment to play with him and then repeat the exercise. This is a great way to introduce your dog to working through distractions as it provides a quick reward for the behavior you desire. It also shows your dog that there is value in ignoring instincts and being faithful to you as his handler. Build upon this exercise over time by conducting other obedience behaviors such as heeling and walking control around the toy. You can also place other toys throughout the area that you will be working in as well.

K9 Bolt - Saxonburg Police Department

When it comes to people, other animals, and noises as distractions it is best to begin conditioning at a distance. Take your time with this process, do not go straight into taking your dog into a store or around large crowds without first conditioning your dog to be in these elements. Find a park or a local outdoor event that people will be at. Take your dog just on the outskirts of one of these locations and conduct some light obedience training that involves lots of play and praise. Have your dog close enough that he can see the people but not so close that he can interact directly with them. Continue this type of training with regular training sessions working your way closer to the distractions with each session. If at any time during your training sessions you find your dog to be overstimulated to the point of constant disobedience, end the session and remove your dog from the area of distractions.

All of the above applies to noises as distractions as well. For instance if you are training your dog to be a hunting dog or a working dog, you will want to slowly introduce gunfire as a distraction in your training. The best practice for this is to conduct training sessions that consist of light obedience and lots of play, with the gunfire being at a distance. Regular training sessions should be conducted with you moving your dog closer to the sound with each session, until he is completely unphased, and remains obedient, when near the source of the sound.

When it comes to introducing distractions, follow the same rule as with any training: never too much too soon. Doing so will allow you to properly condition your dog to many types of distractions. In order to counter an instinctual behavior, you have to provide your dog with something that is of higher value than their natural desire. In the same manner that we teach them to expect a reward for taking action (i.e. sit, down, etc.), we have to teach them to expect a reward for not acting. This is done by creating the scenario that you want to avoid, and then training through it. Think of what situations you and your dog will be in and train specifically for them. This will ensure your dog will be obedient when you need him to be most.

K9 Pori - Halifax County Sheriff's Office

Problem Solving

As mentioned in the disclaimer of this book, the results of canine training will vary with each dog and handler, and with the unique circumstances of any particular incident. Always keep in mind that every action in dog training has the potential to cause a reaction in another area. This is why training has to be continuous for your dog. There is a solution for almost every conceivable problem that you may encounter with your dog. If you find that your dog has developed a problem in a particular area, you should conduct an evaluation of the following areas in order to accurately 'troubleshoot' the cause of the regression:

> **The Handler** - In your case this would be yourself. Consider the following: Have I been conducting regular training sessions with my dog in the area of deficiency? Am I being fair to my dog during training in regards to expectations and corrections? Am I being consistent with my praise and reward for my dog? In the end, every handler gets the dog that they deserve!

> **The Dog** - Has my dog's behavior changed or regressed in other areas? Could my dog be sick or injured? Has my dog been responding appropriately to training in other areas of performance? Are there any environmental factors that could be affecting my dog's performance negatively?

ADVANCED THEORY & PRACTICES 153

> **The Training** - Has the training methods that I have used with my dog been consistent? Is my dog at a point where he could reasonably achieve the goal that I am setting for him, or do I need to break down training to a lower and more appropriate level?

Assessing these areas should greatly assist you in being able to determine a solution for your dog's deficiency. Review this manual and the training instruction for the particular area of deficiency. A lot can be improved with your dog's training simply by going back to the basics. Remember, at the end of the day dog training in its simplest form is rewarding good behavior and correcting bad behavior.

K9 Rocco - Hertford County Sheriff's Office

Chapter Nine

Conclusion

Throughout this book we have covered a vast amount of theory, many practical applications, and a number of training exercises. If you have followed this instruction in the form of a manual as recommended, your dog should have a solid foundation of obedience and you, the handler, should have a number of different tools in your arsenal to be able to successfully train for the desired behavior. Even if there is a behavior that you wish to train your dog for that is not explicitly laid out in this book, the theory, principles, and practice remain the same in your continued training. When it comes to your training, the key is to not stop here at the end of this book. With all of canine training, each of your dog's trained abilities are a perishable skill. This is why it's imperative that you conduct regular consistent training with your dog, no matter their proficiency level.

Training your dog is a commitment that lasts for the lifetime of your partner. Follow through with your commitment completely while always being patient, fair, and consistent. Doing so will create an obedient dog and a lifetime of memories.

K9 Boone - My loyal companion who has had my back on more than one occasion.

Disclaimer

While every effort has been made to ensure that the methods and recommendations contained in this book are sound and accurate, the results of canine training will vary with each dog and handler, and with the unique circumstances of any particular incident. The author does not accept any legal or moral responsibility nor any liability for the outcome of any case or incident, nor for any errors or omissions.

Training Notes

www.ingramcontent.com/pod-product-compliance
Lightning Source LLC
Chambersburg PA
CBHW060502030426
42337CB00015B/1703